ORTHODOXY: FAITH AND LIFE

CHRIST IN THE GOSPELS

ORTHODOXY: FAITH AND LIFE

Volume One
Christ in the Gospels

by
Bishop Gerasimos Papadopoulos

Holy Cross Orthodox Press
Brookline, Massachusetts 02146
1980

Cover design by John Cyril N. Vaporis.

Library of Congress Cataloging in Publication Data

Papadopoulos, Gerasimos.
  Orthodoxy, faith and life.

  Includes index.
  CONTENTS: v. 1. Christ in the Gospels.
  1. Orthodox Eastern Church—Doctrinal and contro-
versial works. I. Title.
BX320.2.P333   230'.19   80-21101
ISBN 0-916586-38-3 (v. 1)
ISBN 0-916586-37-5 (pbk.: v. 1)

PROLOGUE

By the grace of God, I have been serving our Orthodox Church in America for twenty-seven years. Through my many contacts with our faithful, in teaching, in lecturing, and particularly in Bible study groups, I have noted the need for a book that would provide a general yet comprehensive understanding of the person of Christ, of the Church and of the beliefs and hopes of the Christian faith. It is the thirst of our faithful for true knowledge, and their love, which have inspired me to write. Therefore, this series of thoughts on the person and the work of Christ and on the life of the Church is a long overdue obligation to our people.

The purpose of this book is not to exhaust the subject of the Christian faith. Christian truth is so profound and so inexhaustible that, as John rightly commented, if we wanted to write everything about it even the whole world would not be able to contain the books that would be written (Jn. 21.25).

This book is neither a doctrinal nor a critical study of Christian faith. There are already many such good works. Christian truth, which is truth itself, comes from above, from revelation, and is recieved through the heart by intuition. Christian truth is the very mystery of God, of the world and of man, and as such it transcends every critical analysis. Though the person of Christ was revealed to us in history and in the realm of our everyday life, Christ will always lead us to the divine and to the eternal which is the source and the purpose of life and human existence.

When the Apostles tell us something about the person and the work of Christ, they often reveal a completely unfamiliar world which the human mind cannot reach, cannot contain, without the wings of faith. Reason was not meant to be the authentic criterion of truth. The privilege and the responsibility of the mind is to follow the faith which precedes it, to listen as much as it can to the beat of the heart, without forcing it to fit into its own rather narrow confines. The work of the mind is to search together with the heart to find, if possible, God and to worship Him, not to judge Him. Faith is not knowledge, but a meeting. Such a personal encounter with the divine and the eternal as seen in Christ will always be the highest and truest kind of knowledge that man can ever attain. This knowledge is eternal life (Jn. 17.3).

My main purpose is to help the average Christian: to assist the wise to become wiser by studying the Bible on his own or her own and by penetrating more deeply into the mystery of the revelation in Christ. This book also attempts to help the reader feel and live his or her faith more consciously in the worship and life of the Orthodox Church. Faith is life, and faith can be best expressed in the worship of the God in whom we believe.

With faith and worship the heart of a person is enobled and life as an individual person and as a member of the Church is greatly enriched and beautified. Without sublime ideas there is no real life. It was with this spirit in mind that many years ago I wrote my first book as an introduction to the Christian faith. Today, many years later, I am still writing an introduction.

This, then, is the reason why this book was not written as a theological manual or even as a systematic exposition of the Christian faith. Further, it has taken the form of 'a stroll in the garden' of spiritual experience, which has been bequeathed to us by the great ones of faith. I certainly hope and pray that this spiritual experience will also help us all to meet God, to learn how He continues to act in history, and to know ourselves better in His ineffable love in Christ and in the hope of glory which awaits us.

The principle source of this study is the New Testament. As the first written tradition of the Church, the New Testament is always viewed in the light of the life of the Church out of which it emerged and in which faith in Christ is lived. From the New Testament we take only a few select passages. Space does not allow us to touch upon or develop at length all of the passages. The depth and breadth of the Christian faith is immeasureable. Even the Evangelists recorded only a few of the events in the life and work of Christ. Each person is challenged to approach the manifold truth in his or her own way, provided he or she does not distort its majesty and beauty nor deprive it of its inexhaustible richness.

At this point I wish to express my heart-felt thanks to Father Peter A. Chamberas who very graciously undertook to prepare the English translation of my hand-written Greek text and to Presbytera Fotine Stylianopoulos for her invaluable assistance. I also wish to thank all those persons who in various ways have helped in the publication of this book.

Brookline, Mass.
June 13, 1979

Dedicated to the faithful Orthodox Christians
whom I had the privilege of serving

CONTENTS

CHAPTER ONE

RELIGION AND REVELATION

Man has been called a rational being to distinguish him clearly from all other living creatures. But the basic characteristic of rational man is the spiritual one. Man is a spiritual being because he practices religion. From the beginning of time man has believed in god, in a superior being or power, often determined by his own ability to imagine the true transcendent God.

A free and truly spiritual man can never feel at home or be completely satisfied in the created world. He has the tendency to want to break through the boundaries of this narrow world and to soar to some higher, more spiritual, more righteous world. He wants to reach God. There he hopes to find the true light, the real truth, the actual spiritual values of life which alone can make life worthy of its name.

The ancient Greek philosopher Parmenides, whose god was truth, felt the need to advance beyond "the boundaries of the night" in order to receive the revelation of truth. The great philosophers Plato and Aristotle, too, looked beyond our world to find the "true being" the "highest good," the "first immovable mover" who draws all creatures to himself and keeps them alive. Both philosophers knew the beauty and the richness of the physical world. Yet they insisted that the perfect is to be found elsewhere: in the vision of the divine and the eternal. This is why Plato sought an escape from the temporal world, even for a short while, to see heavenly visions and to live with the righteous and the gods in a life of immortality.

The existentialists of our time consider man as the main object of their philosophy, for they see him as a stranger in this finite world; they have observed that man always seeks his existence in communion with something else, somewhere outside of himself (*ex-ist*). Man has the tendency to go beyond the projected boundaries of the visible world. This outward movement is satisfied only when directed toward a personal God who cares personally for him. These are all indications that man is spiritual. The soul of man is created for God and cannot rest until he finds himself near God (Augustine). Even though we are worms and earth our soul seeks the heavenly things (Goethe). All things in the world are symbols which refer us to something higher. Created in the image and likeness of God, man seeks his archetype, his creator, in order to live a whole and spiritual life and to realize his salvation. God is the ultimate spiritual value in the life of man. Whoever denies having any relationship with God also denies his spiritual personality as an individual.

This is why all peoples of all ages have been religious, and have sought to communicate with God. In accordance with the spiritual development of their civilization, they have all wanted to know him and to gain his favor, even though they may not have actually understood him—that unknown God—without the benefit of the revelation of Christ. As St. Paul said to the Athenians: "They should seek God, in the hope that they might feel after him and find him" (Acts 17.27). The following quotation from Plutarch (2nd century A.D.) remains a classical expression of the universality of religion: " If you go around the world you may find towns without walls, without written laws, without money; towns in which there are no schools, gymnasiums, and theatres. But no one has ever seen a town without temples, without god, and without prayers and worship." It is impossible for man to have lived and never to have believed. The history of mankind bears eloquent testimony to the vital spirituality of man.

Many times rationalism has sought to doubt the universality of religion because the object of religion transcends the intellectual capability of the human mind. However, as Romano Guardini would say, this doubt results not so much from the incomprehensibility of faith in God as from intellectual laziness.

Religion is a living experience of the presence of God. This presence imposes requirement and it demands devotion and surrender of man to God as the source of life. The ego of reasoning desires to remain free and resists those demands. The so-called atheists do not take the trouble to listen to the spiritual aspirations of the heart. They raise up the ego as an idol—as god. They, too, after all must have some god to worship! But man does not stand alone in life. He does not live with the nihil of certain existentialists or the drug culture of our time. Existence is communal. True existence is to be found when man lives in communion with God. This is why he seeks God as the source of his existence. In his communion with God who is 'The Being,' one attains a more profound understanding of man—that stranger in this uncertain world.

Religion and Revelation

In essence religion is a living experience of a personal relationship between finite man and the infinite God who in himself is invisible. As such, religion is a mystery that transcends man's merely intellectual capability and belongs to his spiritual experience.

As a relationship between God and man, religion presupposes two things. First, the revelation of the invisible God, and second, the possibility for man to receive such a revelation and to communicate with another, more sublime and more spiritual world. This demonstrates that man is a link between the imminent and the transcendent world. The principle element in man's religion is the revelation of God. Revelation means that God reveals, lets himself be known, to man. Without revelation we cannot speak seriously about religion—regardless of how revelation is made known and how man interprets it according to his cultural environment. In the history of religion we see that God first reveals himself to man. The invisible and transcendent God enters the material world and becomes known to man. God reveals himself to man both indirectly through his nature and directly through personal revelation.

Natural Revelation

First of all God is revealed in nature. Man began to philosophize when he noticed the majesty of the world. From the majesty of natural creation, he began to think about and discern the presence of the creator and provident God. Emmanuel Kant found testimony for the existence of God in the starry

heavens. The revelation of God in nature, however, is somewhat concealed. One must have "eyes to see and ears to hear"
in order to detect the presence of God in the beauty and majesty
of the created world. The Psalmist envisions the universe, senses
the presence of God and begins to sing:

> Bless the Lord, O my soul!...O Lord, how manifold are thy
> works! In wisdom has thou made them all. (Ps.104.1,24)

> The heavens are telling the glory of God; and the firmament
> proclaims his handiwork. (Ps.19.1)

St. Paul tells us that in the beauty of the world we can recognize
the Creator, his infinite power and his divinity (Rom. 1, 19-23).

This is the natural revelation of God which is preceived by
every person who can see, who can understand and who can
interpret well the signs which bear witness to his presence. This
manifestation of God in the world has been regarded as an exodus
of God toward the world. What we see is God manifested in the
economy of creation and salvation of the world. We see the
"energies" of God as they are manifested in the world. The
essence of God in itself we cannot see nor understand. God is so
different from man.

Direct Revelation of God to Man

Besides revealing himself through nature, God also reveals
himself directly to man. Man is created in the image of God and
therefore he can communicate directly with God. God, in a
particular manner, reveals himself to man, the only spiritual
being in the material world. God initiates a sacred dialogue with
man—particularly to certain persons of history. These are the
"elect," the "called," the "selected vessels" of God—great people
who are called by God, or rather because they are called by God
they become great, creating religions and civilizations. They are
pious people who fear God. They thirst for communion with God
"as the hart thirsts after the spring waters"; they live from God
and for God. God reveals Himself and initiates a dialogue with
them revealing his will for the history of the world.

The language of the conversation of man with God is of a
mystical nature; it is the language of the heart. The heart is the

sacred altar where the meeting between God and man takes place and where God reveals himself to all men.

The Religious Experience of Revelation

The experience of the believer at the time of revelation, the time of a meeting with God, is an ineffable and inexpressable mystery. Only those who have had the experience can tell us about it (1 Cor. 2.9, 2 Cor. 12.4). We simply follow the great witnesses of faith. The first thing we realize is that the religious experience is lived as a *personal meeting between God and man.* First God finds man. It is he who first sought out man and said: "Adam where are you?" while Adam was trying to hide. The invisible and transcendent God becomes imminent by entering —in a marvelous way—into the world to communicate with finite man and to make his will known to him. We know God when and to the extent that he reveals himself to us.

God manifests himself as a person, not simply as a being, a power. He presents himself as a person who enters into dialogue with man in an I-thou relationship. Without this experience, this personal encounter with God, we cannot speak of true revelation. Religion without God is inconceivable.

Man responds to God's invitation with faith and a new relationship between God and man is created. It is at this point precisely that religion is born and worship is developed, through which that person will live out his or her relationship with God in accordance with his or her spiritual experience of revelation.

The Experience of the Holy

If we observe the great people of faith when they have their encounter with God, we shall see that they are seized by an 'awefull' feeling before the divine or the holy—to use the language of the Bible. That which distinguishes one religious experience from all other spiritual experiences is precisely the presence of the holy. The holy is what characterizes the absolute perfection of God in contrast to all finite creatures. During revelation man stands before the holy God, the absolute, the "other." Here he senses deeply his smallness, his distance and his dependence upon God. It is to this holiness of God that man kneels reverently rather than to his power. According to R. Otto, who made a special study of religious emotion, the idea of the holy creates in us a double emotion of fear and of fascination, a pull and a push. The holy imposes on the soul a fascination and an aweful fear due to our imperfections. Before God Abraham felt that he was "earth and ashes." Man is so small before God. But he did not cease to desire to be "before the Lord" and to converse with him (Gen. 18.22-33).

Another striking example is given to us by the Prophet Isaiah. When he saw the Lord seated on a throne, high and exalted, and his glory filled the temple, he said:

Woe is me! For I am lost; for I am a man of unclean lips, and I dwell in the midst of a people of unclean lips; for my eyes have seen the King, the Lord of hosts (Is. 6. 5).

But the holy God sent an angel to cleanse the lips and the heart of Isaiah so that he could stand before God and be sent to proclaim God's will to his people.

This sacred love and fear is the religious experience of a cultivated believer. Both go together. Without both of these one cannot talk of true religiosity. "With fear of God, faith, and love come" is the Church's invitation when we are called to approach the holy God for Holy Communion. Fear alone does not constitute religion, but neither can we overlook the chasm which separates us from the holiness of God. It is this harmonious union of love and awe that is missing from so many people today. Many of us still live our religious faith out of fear, while many others do not respect anything that is sacred and holy. We become god and we worship ourselves. Consequently, religion loses its sacredness and people lose the great benefits which true religion can actually offer, as it challenges us to climb ever higher the ladder of moral and spiritual progress, individually and socially, in an ongoing intimate dialogue with God.

Religion is not a creation of man, but of God for the sake of man. It is necessary, however, for man to come to know religion very well and to live it with all of the strength of his soul. No half measures! By being merely lukewarm man is unfair to religion as well as to himself. Religion does not suffer from the so-called unbelievers as much as it suffers from its indifferent believers.

Revelations of God in the Old Testament

At the beginning of creation Adam and Eve were in close communion with God. Sin prompted man to hide, to break his communion. God, however, continued to look after man.

We have another striking revelation in Noah, who was indeed a landmark in the history of mankind. God called Noah. He wanted him to be an instrument to call people to repentence. The people did not listen to him. They followed their own ways, and drowned in the deluge, a symbol for all those who daily perish when they live apart from God. God saved mankind in the faimly of this one "just man" who lived at that time (Gen.6.8-10.17). And thus history continued.

A more particular revelation was the calling of Abraham. God appeared to Abraham and required of him to leave his fatherland and to go wherever God would lead him. God wanted to begin a new people who would be the people of God, a people of faith who would worship God (Gen. 12. 1-3). Abraham obeyed the voice of God and became a symbol of faith and piety. He talked with God, person to person, as a friend to a friend (Gen. 18. 22-33). The mind of man cannot conceive the tremendous faith of Abraham. His life was a life of living faith (Gen. 18. 18-19). Everything for God, even his only son Isaac, for even his son was a gift of God. Thus Abraham became "the father of all who believe," the leader and patriarch of the Hebrew people, from whom Christ came "according to the flesh" (Mt.1.1, Rom.4.11;9. 4-5 Gal. 3.6-19). If we cannot give everything God requires of us, we cannot talk about faith in the living God.

Moses, a truly great man in the Old Testament, was called by God out of the burning bush and was commissioned to liberate Israel from the bondage of slavery in Egypt. He received the Law from God on Mt. Sinai, a law that remains until today a sacred book, both for Hebrews and Christians (Ex. 3. 1-15; 20.1-17).

Call and Commission

Faith and religion are born and developed out of such historical events of divine revelation. As we have seen in the examples mentioned above, God revealed his character and his will for the purpose of the world to certain persons. Those great people who received the revelation came to know God as the Lord of the history of the world and they submitted themselves to him with ab-

solute confidence. Then God armed them with his grace and sent
them to work for the salvation of mankind. They in turn directed
the rest of the people to true faith and to proper worship and life.

This is the way God reveals himself to man. The words of the
prophets are words of God. When read with the eyes of faith one
can see their deeper meaning and can understand how God is
working in history to lead his world to salvation.

The Revelation of God in Christ

In addition to natural revelation and the supernatural direct
revelation to the patriarchs and prophets of the Old Testament,
there is still a third and more sublime revelation of God — the revelation in Christ. In Christ we have a revelation "greater than
that of the prophets"; we have revelation in the Son (Heb. 1
1-2). The revelation in Christ is complete and perfect. "For
in him the whole fullness of the Diety dwells bodily" (Col. 2.
9). He who has seen me has seen the Father (Jn. 14. 8-11).

Christ indeed preached the gospel of the Kingdom of God.
Yet in his person, his life, and particularly the cross, the Apostles
and the pious hearers saw something greater than a prophet and
preacher of the Kingdom of God. They saw the King himself.
They saw the "Holy One" walking among men and women. This is
what St. John means when he says:

> And the Word became flesh and dwelt among us, full of grace
> and truth; we have beheld his glory, glory as of the only Son
> from the Father. (Jn. 1. 14).

Christ is the real revelation of God. The fullness of the experience
of faith surely came after the Resurrection and Pentecost. It was
then that they saw that in Christ, God himself had humbled himself for the salvation of the world (2 Cor. 5. 18-21. Phil. 2. 6-11).
Moreover, the testimony of St. Thomas: "My Lord and my God"
is precisely the conclusion of the Gospel of St. John. Thus in
Christ we have the perfect and final revelation of God, while in the
Christian religion, we have the culmination of the history of religion.

The Experience of the Holy and the Christian Faith

Out of this experience of the holy, which the Apostles had in
the person of Christ, the Christian faith and religion was born.

Christ, the Holy One, as the Apostles knew him during the days of his earthly sojourn, was at the center. Without this experience, it would have been impossible for the Church of Christ to be founded and to be transmitted to the entire world and to remain alive until today and unto eternity. It is from this experience of the Apostles that we can know about the person of Christ, the life of the Church, and the meaning they have for the world.

The Development of the Christian Faith

The Christian faith as it appears in the Gospels is much simpler than what we see today. Faith and religion are an experience, and to the extent that people live them, they develop in external form (as the seed becomes a tree or a child becomes a man). Essentially, however, the Christian faith is the same in the first, in the fourth and in the twentieth century — a religion of redemption and salvation. Such was the basic message of Christ. Christianity was first lived by the Apostles. They were the first eye-witnesses who received the baptism of initiation into the mystery of Christ. This faith and this life they recorded in part in the books of the New Testament. Later the Fathers expressed this same faith and life in doctrines and theological ideas, but primarily they lived it and expressed it as a personal experience in the living language of worship. In the realm of worship the Divine Liturgy will remain for all time the main source from which the faithful can live the experience of the love of God in Christ and in the Holy Spirit.

The Christian Faith in the Twentieth Century

Today the question is raised by many: Does mankind need the Christian faith after so much progress and so many achievements in technology and the sciences? What role can religion play in the life of contemporary man?

Religion is necessary for the wholeness of the human personality. The religious experience is an *a priori* factor in man which needs an opportunity to be expressed, to be lived, no matter what age one lives in, or what position one holds in society. Today, much more than in other periods of time, we need the Christian faith. As the scientific and technological achievements of man become greater and greater, man becomes increasingly aware of his smallness, his weakness, and his loneliness before the infinite world he is discovering. We have learned so many things about the world within. Proof of this is the problematic question for man posed by the modern existentialist philosophy. Even the presence of the cults in our time, despite the serious questions they raise, bear testimony that man needs religion to live a more whole life.

Only faith, only the religious experience of our personal relationship with God, can speak to us about man. In other words, only God can speak authentically about his image. He alone knows us. And in the religious life we learn that he indeed knows us and loves us and is concerned about us we are something special for him (1 Cor. 8. 2-3; Gal. 4. 6-9).

The religious experience also tells us that man is by nature religious. Man is never content with mere food and clothing. He is "greater than all these." Man seeks to go beyond himself, to break the barriers which surround him. He seeks something greater in order to live. He seeks the spiritual values of truth, virtue, good and beauty. At the pinnacle of these values stands always the value of religion, of the divine, of the holy. All values ultimately lead to the divine. Toward this desired good of the soul, man is ever drawn both consciously and unconsciously. The more religious life is developed and the soul united with the divine, the more it is refined in all of its aspects. When someone encounters God he cannot but live a "godly life," as the Stoics used to say.

The religiosity of man is a reality and a truth that is not proven by sheer logic. It cannot be imposed from the outside. Each person must live in himself the experience of his encounter with God, as was the case with the great men and women of faith. This is a possibility we all possess, for we are the "image of God," particularly if we could but leave our heart free as we read a book, or whisper a prayer alone or with others.

The perfect and final revelation of God was in the person and work of Jesus Christ. In Christ, God truly "visited his people" and spoke personally to man. According to Hebrews 1. 1-2:

> In many and various ways God spoke of old to our fathers by the prophets; but in these last days he has spoken to us by a Son...

And according to St. John, the eternal Son and Word of God
became flesh and dwelt among us, full of grace and truth; we

have beheld his glory, glory as of the only Son from the Father.
(1. 14)

In the person of Christ, God himself came and spoke to man person to person ". . . that is, in Christ God was reconciling the world to himself . . ." (2 Cor. 5.19).

This revelation in Christ was experienced primarily by the persons who lived near him, who heard his teaching and who saw his glory throughout his life and especially in his death on the cross and his resurrection from the dead. Enlightened by the Holy, they recognized Christ as Savior of the world, as Lord and as God, and as such they preached him to the world and founded the Christian Church.

These experiences of faith which the Apostles had have been preserved in part in the four Gospels and in the Epistles of the apostles. There are twenty-seven books in the New Testament. These were written between 50 and 100 A.D. and all together they constitute the *Evangelion* – the Good News of God for the Salvation of the world in Christ. We call this collection of books the New Testament because it represents the new covenant, the new agreement which God has made for the salvation of the world in the person of Christ.

These books are written in the language of faith. They are not mere theoretical teachings. They presuppose the faith of the Church and they are written to lead us to faith. They are not written as historical accounts to be read with the questions of historical and literary criticism, though they do refer to historical events. The language of the New Testament presupposes from its very first lines faith in the divinity and lordship of the Savior Jesus Christ. The Gospel is from the outset the "Gospel of Jesus Christ," as the Church believes and lives Christ," as the Church believes and lives Christ with the proclamation of the Apostles and with the daily worship of the Church. The Gospels are "commentaries," notations which remind us of certain elements in the life and the teaching of Christ and of the Christian Church. Only the life of the Church can give us the real meaning of the various expressions in the New Testament. The life of the Church is the background against which the New Testament was written and against which it can be best understood. Moreover, the Gospel is really a possession of the Church; it was written *by* the Church and *for* the Church.

Consequently, those who are not initiated into the Church can never fully understand the mystery of Christ in all its depth and height and breadth (cf. Eph. 3. 1-19).

In the books of the New Testament, when properly studied in the light of the continuing history of the Church, a Christian can see what faith in Christ really is. For it is "the preaching of the Apostles and the doctrines of the Fathers that have made firm the one faith" and the Church correctly teaches and glorifies the mystery of our faith (Sunday of Orthodoxy).

CHAPTER TWO

THE BEGINNING

The Geneology of Jesus Christ

"The book of the geneology of Jesus Christ, the son of David, the son of Abraham" Mt. 1. 1, "the son of Adam the son of God" Lk. 3. 38.

The four Evangelists give us the faith in Christ in life situation settings that are more or less in historical order. Their purpose is to present the Christ of faith as the Church knows Him. They describe the life of Christ mainly from his Baptism to his Ascension. Matthew and Luke offer some additional information about the ancestry and birth of Christ. This information is not merely historical data, but also an introduction to the faith in Christ. It is an introduction to the Gospel, but it is also the Gospel itself in summary form.

The Gospels presuppose the faith of those who wrote them and of those who will read them. When the Gospels were being written, during the second half of the first century, faith in Christ had already been established in the Church. Consequently the Evangelists wrote freely. Their language is the language of the faith, the piety and the expectations of the people of their time, but it is always illumined by the faith in Christ as the entire Church lived it. It is only when the Gospels are read with the faith of the Church that they offer us all of the depth and the majesty of divine revelation in a complete unity, with the person of Christ as the beginning, the middle and the end.

This is what Matthew means when he writes,

> The book of the geneology of Jesus Christ
> the son of David, the son of Abraham.

Abraham is the one who first received the promises of God in revelation (Gen. 12. 1-2, 17.19). David is the king *par excellence* of
Israel to whom God promised the Messiah (2 Sam. 7.12; Ps. 132.
11). The Jewish people believed in general that the Messiah would
be of the "seed" of Abraham and more specifically a descendent
of King David (Rom. 1.3, 3.13, Gal. 3.16, Mk. 12.35). By con-
necting Christ with Abraham and David, Matthew unites the revelation of God in the Old Testament with the revelation in the New
Testament and thus establishes the continuity of the whole of revelation as well as the history of the world. In Christ we have the
fulfillment of the promises of the Old Testament and the apex of
divine revelation.

Luke broadens this pre-history Christ to present him as "the
son of Adam, the son of God" and thus to unite him with the history and the destiny of the whole world (Lk. 3. 23-38). Revelation takes place in history, but it also creates history. In the revelation in Christ we also have the revelation of the meaning of history.

John, with his "In the beginning was the Word...and the Word
was God," soars behind the history of the world to that eternal
Being of God. But he also moves beyond history to see us all united with Christ in eternity (Jn. 1. 1, 17. 24). This is how the eye-
witnesses, the Apostles, saw Christ and that is how they present
him to us in the Gospels: the Son and Word of God by whom all
things were made and through whom all are saved. Accordingly,
Christ in the New Testament is not approached as a man, but as
God incarnate for the salvation of the world.

With this faith and with the Bible open before us, let us now
take a spiritual walk in the garden of these sacred writings, so that
we, too, may feel and live, the mystery of our salvation in Christ,
as an act of God's love for us.

The Birth of John the Baptist
Luke 1.5-17

Luke, as an historian, seeks to present to us the Gospel in as
much an historical order as possible. He wants to give us the Christ
of faith, "the truth concerning the things of which you have been
informed" (Lk. 1. 1-4). This is why he writes about the persons
who played an important role in presenting Christ to the world —

his All-Holy Mother and John the Baptist.

The birth of John (the Baptist) is miraculous, a gift of God in answer to the prayers of Zechariah and Elizabeth. The angel Gabriel announced the birth of John. Zechariah had difficulty in believing, and for this reason he became speechless. And indeed what could one have said in words about such an announcement! The person and the mission of John is great, and closely connected with the revelation of God in Christ. And such great things usually require silence. The Virgin Mary, the *Panagia*, too, does not seem to have talked to Joseph about her annunciation. She left everything to God.

Zechariah remained silent until the promise was fulfilled. Then his tongue was loosed and he praised the Lord God for his mercy toward Israel and he prophesied about the mission of the child, according to the words of the angel and the expections of the Jewish people (Lk. 1. 13-17. 64-80). John grew up in the desert preparing himself for the hour when God would call him to his task. The desert was and is always appropriate for spiritual preparation.

The Annunciation to the Theotokos
Luke 7.26-56

The Evangelist Luke especially has preserved in his Gospel certain fine details of the Annunciation to the Theotokos and the Birth of Christ. Apocryphal Gospels, which the Church does not accept as authentic, speak to us about the birth of Panagia and her entrance into the Temple. At this point we have to emphasize that all the accounts pertaining to the Theotokos are given directly or indirectly by the Theotokos herself who kept these things as treasures in her maternal heart. Here again the criterion is faith and not the mind of man. The mind, of course has its place but here its place is to marvel at the Mystery and not to analyze or explain it. It is faith which helps us to somehow understand how Mary narrated these accounts, how they were preserved by the faithful, and how they inspired the Evangelist to record them for our own edification

In the sixth month the angel Gabriel was sent from God to a city of Galilee named Nazareth, to a virgin betrothed to a man whose name was Joseph, of the house of David; and the virgin's name was Mary. And he came to her and said,"Hail, O favored one, the Lord is with you!" (Jn.1.26-28).

Again the angel Gabriel is sent by God. He brings a strange message-greeting. The Virgin is troubled. The same thing happened with Zechariah, and later with the shepherds. When the divine is revealed to us, it troubles us because it is the Holy, the 'wholly other,' the completely different, which comes to us from other worlds which are foreign to our own small world. The angel, therefore comforts her:

> And the angel said to her, 'Do not be afraid, Mary, for you have found favor with God. And behold, you will conceive in your womb and bear a son, and you shall call his name Jesus. He will be great, and will be called the Son of the Most High; and the Lord God will give to him the throne of his father David, and he will reign over the house of Jacob for ever; and of his kingdom there will be no end' (Lk.1.30-35).

The conception is the work of God fulfilled by the Holy Spirit. And the holy child to be born will be called the Son of God. He will sit on the throne of David and will continue to fulfill the history of the people of God.

When the Angel had assured her that the entire miracle was the will of God, Mary replied,"I am the handmaid of the Lord; let it be to me according to your word." This answer was the opposite of what Eve did in the beginning. Our Church has composed some of the most beautiful hymns for the Annunciation to the Theotokos, which is the beginning of the mystery of salvation. Often a contrast is made between the obedience of Mary to the will of God and the disobedience of Eve. The one was cursed and the other was highly favored. Through her human curiosity Eve disobeyed a commandment of God, and sin and death entered into the world. With her faith, humility and free obedience to the will of God, Mary became the Mother of the Savior Christ; she became *Theotokos.*

Mary Visits Elizabeth
Luke 1.39-56

In this visitation we have the first impressions of this double an-

nunciation. The language of Elizabeth and especially the doxology of Mary are a lyrical poem which shows us the beauty and the
magnificence of the thought of the faithful of that time. Both women believe that "the Child" will be the expected Messiah, the
Savior and Lord. They glorify God who will bring, through the
Messiah, justice and peace to Israel and the entire world. God will
exhalt the humble who suffer in life and he will humble the rulers
and the rich who exploit the people of God (cf. 1 Sam.2.1-10).

With Zechariah's hymn (1.68-79), Luke closes this introductory
section and proceeds to describe the birth of Christ.

The Role of Joseph
Matthew 1.18-25

At this point Matthew preserves for us a few details about Joseph
which complete the picture of the annunciation. He tells us that
Joseph was troubled when he saw Mary pregnant. God, however,
reassured him and consequently Joseph took the Virgin Mother
and the Child under his protection. This is the reason why he was
considered "the father of the Child" without, of course, being so
in fact (Lk.3.23).

With the birth of the Child, the prophecy of Isaiah was to be
fulfilled:

'Behold, a virgin shall conceive and bear a son, and his name
shall be called Emmanuel' (which means, God with us). Mt.1.
23.cf.Is.4.14)

Matthew sees the divine revelation as a unified whole. In the person of Christ, he sees fulfilled all the prophecies of the Old Testament and all the promises of God to Israel. Therefore, at every
marvelous event in the life of Jesus, he sees the fulfilment of some
prophecy or some hope of Israel, even if the prophecy does not refer directly to Christ (cf.Mt.2.15).

The Birth of Christ
Luke 2.1-20; Matthew 2.1-12

Here, too, Luke describes with greater detail the historical con-
text in which Christ was born. He ties the birth of Christ to the
world-dominance of Rome. In contrast to Augustus, Christ is pre-

sented as the new king who will conquer the world with divine love. This is how the Church chants at the Vespers of Christmas:

When Augustus reigned alone upon earth,
The many kingdoms of men came to an end;
And when Thou wast made man of the pure Virgin
The many Gods of idolatry were destroyed.
The cities of the world passed under one single rule;
And the nations came to believe in one sovereign Godhead.
Great is thy mercy, O Lord, glory to thee.

The Birth of Christ
Luke 2.8-20

Luke presents us with a very simple account of the birth of Christ. But everything is very striking for those who have lived the life of travelers with humble lodgings. The birth takes place in a cave, a manger. God always reveals himself in a humble, somewhat concealed manner for he does not wish to violate man's freedom. He seeks man's heart, and the pure heart can discern the great even in its humble appearance; it can receive within itself the great, the divine, God himself. Without the heart, all things remain small and impoverished in our lives. We, too, remain small and poor, no matter how high it may appear we have risen if we do not have a pure heart.

Even though the birth of Christ took place under humble and obscure circumstances, there was no lack of witnesses to the divine event. The angels who are always in the presence of God's throne brought the message to the suffering earth: "Glory to God in the highest, and on earth peace." It is this peace which will always fill our hearts as we believe and celebrate the event. First of all the simple shepherds heard the angels singing of the divine event and they hastened to worship. The Magi, too, found out about Christ from the star and traveled to worship him and to offer him gifts as king. We could say that the Magi and the shepherds became the first Christians. "Blessed are the poor in spirit...the pure in heart, for they shall see God." People today still decorate the Christmas crèche with the figures of the shepherds and the Magi who beckon us to offer ourselves to Christ who will fill us with the joy and peace which flows from his divine love.

The Circumcision and the Presentation of the
Child in the Temple
Luke 2.21-39

Christ was born in a Jewish environment, and Luke with particular attention follows his life according to the spirit of the Mosaic Law. Thus Christ received circumcision on the eighth day (Gen.17) and was given the name Jesus as the archangel Gabriel predicted.

On the fortieth day, "Joseph and Mary took him to Jerusalem to present him to the Lord." This was the ancient practice of the Jews to dedicate the first-born children to God as an expression of gratitude to him for sparing their children from death in Egypt (Ex.12-13; Lev.12).

Many people were probably in the Temple on that day when Jesus was presented. But the Spirit of God again separated two witnesses of the event—Simeon and Anna. Both were righteous and devout, "awaiting for the consolation of Israel." They were awaiting the coming of the Messiah—the Savior. The Holy Spirit had revealed to Simeon that he would live to see the Messiah. And when he saw the child Jesus, he recognized him as the expected Messiah. Simeon took Jesus in his arms and glorified God saying:

'Lord, now lettest thou thy servant depart in peace, according to thy word; for mine eyes have seen thy salvation which thou has prepared in the presence of all peoples, a light for revelation to the Gentiles, and for glory to thy people Israel.' (Lk.2. 29-32)

Simeon, however, predicted that Christ, the light to the Gentiles and the glory of Israel, "was destined to cause the falling and rising of many in Israel." Many were to rise and many were to fall according to the position they would take toward the person of Christ. Even His Mother would experience much pain, which she did especially at the crucifixion of her Son.

The *Nyn Apolyis* of Simeon is repeated by our Church at the end of every Vesper Service, and by the priest to himself at the end of every Liturgy to reassure us that in going to church and in worship we have seen with the eyes of our soul the Savior Lord; we have talked with him and now we leave filled with peace and spiritual joy. We can consider our church attendance a failure if we do not experience this emotion.

The Visit of the Magi. The Escape to Egypt.
The Return to Nazareth
Matthew 2.1-23

The Magi were wise men from the east who studied the appearances and movements of stars and connected these with the births
of great men. In the appearance of a large star or a combination of
stars they discerned that some great king was born who could be
the Messiah the Jewish people awaited. This is why they went to
Jerusalem and asked "where is he who has been born king of the
Jews? for we saw his star in the East, and have come to worship
him" (Mt.2.2). Herod, the king who reigned there was disturbed.
The theologians of Israel ascertained that the Messiah would be
born in Bethlehem of Judea. Micah the prophet had foretold this
(5.1-3). Herod decided to kill the child. The Magi went to Bethlehem, worshiped the child and offered him gifts of gold, incense,
and myrrh. Because of a dream they had they did not return
to Herod to tell him about the child, but they departed to their
own country "by another way" (Mt. 2.3-12). Then Herod ordered
the cruel killing of the infants in the hope that among them
would be Jesus the King of the Jews. But God, who provides all
things, directed Joseph to leave immediately for Egypt with Mary
and the child. He did so and they lived there until the death of Herod. Later they returned to "the land of Israel . . . and dwelt in a
city called Nazareth" (Mt. 1.10-23). Matthew remembers at this
point two prophecies which he freely relates to the person of Jesus Christ: "Out of Egypt I called my son" (Hosea 11.1), and "He
will be called a Nazarene" (Mt. 2.23).

Jesus as a Twelve-year Old Boy
Luke 2.40-52

Very little has been preserved by the Evangelists regarding the
childhood years of Jesus. In just one verse Luke describes how the
Child grew up near his parents "and became strong, filled with wisdom, and the favor of God was upon him" (2.10).

When the child Jesus was twelve years old the holy family took
part in the annual pilgrimage for Passover in Jerusalem. In all prob-
ability this may have been the first time Jesus went to Jerusalem

for a Passover Feast. What he felt during those days of his stay in the sacred center of Judaism, what he saw or heard from the rabbis and preachers on the great Passover Feast, no one can say. Luke only tells us that the child was separated from his parents and remained in the courtyard of the Temple. Perhaps at the time of their departure for their return home, some conversation of the great teachers of Israel attracted young Jesus and, forgetting himself, he remained in the Temple "among the teachers." He asked questions but also gave answers himself. "And all who heard him were amazed at his understanding and his answers" (2.47). When after three days his mother and Joseph found him in the Temple, they asked why he had done such a thing and caused them such anxiety. His answer was brief, polite and firm: 'How is it that you sought me? Did you not know that I must be in my Father's house?' (2.49).

The words of Luke are so carefully chosen that we are led to believe that in this child the divine is revealed, that this child has a divine origin. The child's answer to his parents shows that he considered himself to be the Son of God in a particular way. Luke notes that "they did not understand the saying which he spoke to them" (2.50). His parents did not understand the meaning of his words, nor did they ask for any further explanation. Whatever they were thinking must have been in accordance with the dreams and expectations of the Jewish people for their Messiah—a powerful king who would liberate his nation. This is how Zechariah, too, saw the Messiah (1.68-72).

The revelation of God is oftentimes not direct and in all its fullness. Finite man cannot receive divine revelation directly. God told Moses that "you cannot see my face, for no one may see me and live" (Ex.33.20). The divine is revealed secretly under the veil of nature. We see the glory of God in the "cloud" or behind the "rock," or in the "cool breeze." God appears in the form of an "angel," or in the form of a "servant." He becomes flesh and dwells among us (Jn.1.14. Phil.1.6-11). To see the divine, one needs "eyes that see." He must be either wiser than Plato and the Magi, or very simple—"poor in spirit," as were the shepherds, Simeon and Anna.

Thus divine revelation unfolds naturally in the world in general and in the life of each person in particular. Our whole life is nothing other than a gradual revelation of the divine in us. Perfect knowledge of God coincides with the perfection of human life, and this, precisely, is the eternal life (Jn.17.3).

The Word became flesh and the mystery was discerned only by a few — the shepherds, the Magi, Simeon, Anna, and Joseph. With a mother's intuition, Mary understood this mystery a little better than the others, but even she "treasured all these things in her heart" in sacred silence (2.51). Only after the Resurrection, when the entire mystery was revealed, did she speak about it directly or indirectly to Luke, so that he in turn could preserve it for us. And he indeed preserved it for us in one sentence: "And Jesus grew in wisdom and stature, and in favor with God and man" (2.52). With this one verse, Luke again leaves us to imagine for ourselves the full development of the child until the day when his public ministry would begin. The hour of revelation is not impatient. It is regulated only by God and God works in eternity. For us there is only patience and prayer.

This introductory picture of the conception and birth of Christ together with the signs revealed in Jerusalem, remove somewhat the veil covering the mystery of his divinity so that we can follow Christ more easily through his public ministry and draw for ourselves certain conclusions about his Person. Even during his public ministry, the divinity of Christ is always shown indirectly, veiled and in accordance with the ability of people to look upon the divine. In his every word, in his every deed, he will challenge us to recognize him and to believe that indeed he is "the Christ, the Son of the living God" (Mt.16.16).

Myth and Divine Reality

Some of the accounts which the Evangelists have preserved for us regarding the person of Christ might appear at first glance to be 'mythological' and our small minds can sometimes be scandalized. And if our faith does not have strong foundations we can fall. Famous Protestant theologians have thought in recent years that they could "de-mythologize" some of the New Testament account, but without any success. The divine must be approached with absolute faith, a child-like faith; one has to delve more deeply in order to approach the breadth, the length, the height and the depth of the mystery which is hidden behind the accounts and which at first glance may appear to be 'myth.' All great and extra-ordinary things convey a sense of the 'fabulous,' i.e. mythical— they are so great that one cannot comprehend them with the mind alone. If we could see a flower, how it is formed, and how it grows with its manifold colors and delicate aroma, we could say that it is a fable—reality that talks to us about God. If God has ever re-vealed himself to us through nature, and he has, he has done so through the person of Christ. This is why the manner by which Christ came to us appears to be 'mythical'—transcending by far our finite understanding.

CHAPTER THREE

ST. JOHN THE FORERUNNER AND THE
BEGINNING OF THE GOSPEL OF JESUS CHRIST

In the fifteenth year of the reign of Tiberius Caesar . . . the word of God came to John the son of Zechariah in the wilderness: and he went into all the region about the Jordan, preaching a baptism of repentance for the forgiveness of sins. As it is written in the book of the words of Isaiah the prophet,

"The voice of one crying in the wilderness:
Prepare the way of the Lord,
make his paths straight.
Every valley shall be filled,
and every mountain and hill shall
be brought low,
and the crooked shall be made straight,
and the rough ways shall be made smooth;
and all flesh shall see the salvation of God"
(Lk.3.1-6).

According to Luke, divine revelation clearly takes its place within political history. History itself is but the various stations of revelation. And for the manifestation of the Messiah all things had been prepared from above. The thirst for a Messiah-Savior had reached its most intensive point in Israel as well as in the whole world. The Roman Empire had united the world around the Mediterranean Sea. With Alexander the Great the thirst of the Greek spirit for truth became the thirst of the whole world. The people of Israel were ready. The Prophet Isaiah had foretold the coming of the Savior-Judge (40.1-11). The Prophet Micah foresaw the forerunner of the Messiah in the form of another Elijah. The main subject in the conversations and the prayers of the contemporary Jews was the coming of the Messiah.

In such an atmosphere of anticipation John the Baptist appeared. As Mark 1.5 characteristically emphasizes, "all the country of Judea, and all the people of Jerusalem went out to him." In the person of John with his austere, prophetic preaching of repentance, the people saw the Messiah, or at least, his forerunner Elijah. John assured the people: "I am not the Christ...I came baptizing with water..."; the Christ,"the Lamb of God, who takes away the sin of the world!" (Jn.1.19-34) "He will baptize you with the Holy Spirit" (Mk.1.7-8).

John was truly the forerunner of the Messiah, and the great spiritual movement which he engendered with his preaching of repentance marked the hour for the Christ to appear in Israel and to begin his work of salvation (cf. Mk.9.11-13).

The Baptism

"Then Jesus came from Galilee to the Jordan to John to be baptized by him" (Mt.3.13).

Enlightened by the Holy Spirit, John recognized in the person of Jesus the anticipated Messiah and hesitated to baptize Him. "How can the servant put his hand on the Master?" as the Church hymn expresses it. But Jesus insisted that this is proper for those whose mission it is to fulfill all of the commandments of God. And as we have seen, even the baptism by John was the commandment and the will of God. John finally consented and baptized Jesus. Jesus was baptized out of love toward the people, as a representative of all mankind. Together with him all mankind was mystically baptized and saved. However, the perfect act of salvation was to take place on the Cross.

The Theophany

And when Jesus was baptized, he went up immediately from the water, and behold, the heavens were opened and he saw the Spirit of God descending like a dove, and alighting on him; and lo, a voice from heaven, saying, 'This is my beloved Son, with whom I am well pleased.' (Mt.3.16-17)

As soon as Jesus came up out of the water, a theophany oc-

curred; the presence of God was manifested in a visible form.
Something like an opening occurred in the sky and the Holy Spirit
in a visible manner, like a dove, descended and rested on Jesus. At
the same time the voice of the Father above was heard witnessing
that he who was baptized was the Beloved Son of God. In Christ
God was pleased to save the world, to transfigure it and to restore
in man the image of God which had been lost since the time of the
fall.

The revelation of God here became more clear and direct. The
Son was baptized below. The Spirit descended from above and the
heavenly Father bore witness to the Son. Jesus is the Beloved Son,
the anticipated Messiah, and through the Holy Spirit He was dedicated to the work of Salvation.

The symbolic opening of the heavens is a sign of the new communion between heaven and earth, between God and man. The appearance of the Holy Spirit as a dove is the symbol of peace between God and man, which begins with the person and work of
Christ. "Peace on earth, good will to men."

The Temptations
Matthew 4.1-11; Luke 4.1-13

The Son of God became man; "He became flesh and dwelt
among us." And man is tempted. Yes the tempter is at liberty to
tempt a free man and indeed does tempt him especially when he
is about to begin some good task. The Fathers say that the devil
is envious of the good. The form and the language of temptation is
not known to all of us. We do know, however, its method. The devil always seeks to mislead man away from God, and, if possible,
to bring him in opposition to God. When one is not near God, he
can easily turn against God. He seeks to take the place of God by
force. This is how we saw temptation in Paradise at the beginning
of the creation of the world. Satan promised Adam that he would
become like God if he could only disobey the will of God. And
Holy Scripture notes: "Then the eyes of both of them were
opened, and they knew they were naked" (Gen.3.4-7).

Here Satan will try to tempt Jesus himself, the New Adam, at
the beginning of salvation, at the beginning of the new creation.
The temptations of Jesus, as they are expressed, presuppose in Je-

sus the consciousness that he is the God-sent Messiah—Savior of the world, the founder of the Kingdom of God on earth. The strategy of Satan is to make Jesus seek the kingdom for himself, without God, and to give the Kingdom of God the color of the kingdom of this world, the color of power and show.

For forty days Jesus was guided by the Spirit in the desert. He ate nothing. His mind was on God and on his work. Finally, he felt hunger. And the tempter found the opportunity to begin his temptations. "If you are the Son of God, tell these stones to become bread." The temptation is a powerful one. All of mankind is struggling for its "bread." The Messiah was expected by the people with the hope that he would provide them with food, among other things. Jesus, however, resisted temptation. No! Bread is not everything in man's life. God himself had said this to Moses: "Man does not live on bread alone but that man lives by everything that proceeds out of the mouth of the Lord" (Deut.8.3). During the forty days Jesus lived on the word of God. Thus he overcame the first temptation.

After this first temptation, Satan challenged Jesus to do an extraordinary miracle—to throw himself down from a cliff to show that he is the Son of God. In this instance, too, the answer was ready: "Again it is written, 'You shall not tempt the Lord your God' (Mt.4.7; Deut.6.16). It is not right to force God to do miracles for us when there is no real need.

The final temptation came as a promise. Jesus knew that he was the Messiah-King. So Satan projected the whole world as if it were his and promised to turn it over to Jesus, if Jesus would only do one small thing—bow down and worship Satan. This is the greatest temptation—to win the whole world with only one word. Here, too, Jesus resisted the temptation. "Begone, Satan! for it is written: 'You shall worship the Lord your God, and him only shall you serve'," (Mt.4.10; Deut.6.13). Man follows God only and him alone does he worship. Only from God does man seek and receive the good things of life. In this manner Christ conquered the tempter. And the Evangelists describe this victory very beautifully: " Then the devil left him, and behold, the angels came and ministered to him" (Mt.4.11). This is the victory against Satan. Luke, however, knows that Satan will not rest. This is why he adds "the devil...departed from him until an opportune time" (Lk.4.13).

The final victory over Satan was to take place on the Cross.

Satan will always seek to catch man at three basic points: at man's natural needs of the body, at man's desire for self-aggrandizement, and at man's love of worldly power. Christ resisted confidently all three. He put before everything else the will of God and with this he overcame all the temptations.

The question for us is this: Do we really *know* the will of God? It is only when we really know that the will of God is always for the good of man that we can resist the temptations in our lives which always push us toward evil and away from God. The practical means to combat such temptations are: faith, patience, prayer and fasting.

The First Disciples
John 1.29-57

Immediately after the temptations, the Synoptic Gospels [the three Gospels of Matthew, Mark and Luke are called Synoptic because they have so much material in common that we can read them together in parallel columns] present the imprisonment of John the Baptist, possibly because they want to introduce us directly to the work of Jesus in Galilee. The fourth Evangelist, however, has preserved in his Gospel certain events which occured before the imprisonment of John. John is writing his Gospel twenty to thirty years after the other three Gospels were written. The faith in Christ is by now well established in the life of the Church. This is why John omits some events from the life of Christ recorded by the Synoptics and includes in his Gospel other events and thus somehow completes the evangelical history. The theological manner with which John presents the acts and words of Christ helps us to penetrate more deeply into the mystery of salvation in Christ. This, after all, is the purpose of the Gospels, namely faith (Jn.20. 30).

The First Testimony of John for Christ
John 1.35-42

In this section John describes how Jesus called his first disciples. It is a very moving moment. Probably soon after the temptations Jesus passed before John the Baptist and his disciples. John pointed out Jesus to his disciples and said "Behold, the Lamb of God, who takes away the sin of the world!" This is the first testimony of John for Christ. The Evangelist John is interested in all of the events which lead to some testimony either from men or from Christ himself or even from the Father.

When Jesus passed by again two disciples of the Baptist followed him. One was Andrew and the other, of course, was John who wrote the account of this incident. They stayed with Jesus for about two hours. They got to know a little about him, and Jesus apparently revealed himself to them. First, Andrew found Peter, his brother, and reported to him with joy: "We have found the Messiah," and then he brought his brother to Jesus. This is the greatest 'Eureka' of man. Later Jesus found Philip and called him to follow him. Philip in turn found Nathaniel and told him, "We have found him of whom Moses in the Law and also the prophets wrote, Jesus of Nazareth, the son of Joseph" (Luke writes, "being the son (as was supposed) of Joseph." Lk. 3.23). Nathaniel, however, doubted. But Philip told him "come and see." And he came and saw and believed and confessed: "Rabbi, you are the Son of God! You are the King of Israel!" (Jn. 1.49).

This is the way faith is transmitted. We find, we see, we believe strongly in Christ and then we call others to him: a brother calls his brother, a friend calls his friend to share the treasure we have found. But in order to find him we must search, we must thirst for him, we must knock. Without our effort we cannot find anything, much less can we find the divine.

After this, John describes certain incidents in the life of Christ which little by little reveal his personality and his divine character.

The Wedding in Cana
John 2.1-11

The first miracle which the Gospels have recorded was done on the joyous occasion of a wedding in Cana. Jesus turned water into "good wine" to help in the joy of life and to show us the wealth of grace he came to bring us.

The words he spoke to his mother: "O woman, what have you to do with me?" should not seem strange to us. They simply indicate that the time when Christ begins his work, and consequently the miracles, is not dependent upon men but upon God himself who sent him to this work.

This miracle, like all the miracles, John saw as a 'sign' which reveals in practical terms the glory of the Son and challenges one to believe in him. This is exactly how the narrative ends: "He thus revealed in his glory, and his disciples saw the glory of Christ as Lord of nature and as full of love for man."

The First Trip to Jerusalem
John 2.12-25

After the miracle at Cana, John takes us to Jerusalem for the Passover Feast. Jesus saw there the temple, "his father's house," turned into a "house of business." He had seen it quite differently when he was twelve years old. The temple had become a means to exploit the greed of men and greed ultimately completely destroys the spirituality of man. Righteous indignation overcame Jesus and he found the strength to throw everyone and everything out of the temple. Noone was there to stop him, for the people saw clearly the divine power in his movements.

This was Jesus' first conflict with the leaders and with wealth. This conflict was to eventually lead him to the Cross. He predicted this very fact when he said: "Destroy this temple, and I will raise it again in three days." Only after the Resurrection did the disciples realize that by temple Jesus meant his own body, his death and resurrection.

The Meeting With Nicodemos
John 3.1-21

On this first trip of his public ministry to Jerusalem, the political and religious center of Judaism, Jesus found no serious faith, and he "did not entrust himself to them" (2.24); he did not open his heart to them. John, however, describes one unique meeting between Jesus the lawgiver and Nicodemos, the teacher of the Law. Nicodemos went to Jesus at night to have a dialogue with him in the stillness of the night. In this narrative some things come from the mouth of Nicodemos and some from the mouth of Jesus and still others from the faith of the Evangelist—all of these together give us a general outline of the entire mystery of Salvation in Christ. We need, however, to have the faith of the Church in mind in order to draw from the passage the truth in all its depth. John wrote his Gospel with the faith and the life of the Church in mind, leaving many things to be understood as already familiar.

The subject of the dialogue is entrance into the kingdom of God and eternal life. This was the nostalgic desire of the times: How can one enter the kingdom of God? The answer is one: only with a real rebirth by the Holy Spirit. "Truly, truly, I say to you, unless one is born anew, he cannot see the kingdom of God... unless one is born of water and Spirit, he cannot enter the kingdom of God" (3.3,5). How the Holy Spirit works this rebirth is a mystery. But we do know that the Spirit will come to the Church after the Son of Man is "lifted up" that is, when Christ is raised upon the Cross. Before Christ was glorified through the Cross "the Spirit had not been given" (Jn.7.39). This raising up of Christ for the salvation of the world was prefigured by the bronze serpent which Moses raised in the desert. "And as Moses lifted up the serpent in the wilderness, so must the Son of man be lifted up, that whoever believes in him may have eternal life" (3.13-14).

The "Son of man" is the principle title for the Messiah. Christ used this title many times in the third person when he wanted to say that he himself was the Messiah. The Son of God is called the "Son of man" because he became man for the salvation of mankind. The Prophet Daniel (7.13) first envisioned the Messiah as a "Son of man." Since then it has become the main title for the Messiah.

"For God so loved the world that he gave his one and only Son, that whoever believes in him should not perish but have eternal life" (Jn.3.16). This is the mystery of Salvation—the infinite love of God. The love of God for man is so great that God offered His Son to be sacrificed for the salvation of mankind. Man himself needs to offer in return faith in this love of God and a virtuous life. Faith and virtue develop together. An evil person cannot believe; faith is coming close to God, and a person who sins cannot come close to God who is Light. This very principle is emphasized by John in his entire Gospel: Christ came to the world as the Light and man by free choice did not want to see the Light; he preferred the darkness. Man does not believe and this attitude of disbelief becomes God's judgement on him.

> For God sent the Son into the world, not to condemn the
> world, but that the world might be saved through him. He
> who believes in him is not condemned; he who does not be-
> lieve is condemned already, because he has not believed in the
> name of the only Son of God. And this is the judgement, that
> the light has come into the world, and men loved darkness
> rather than light, because their deeds were evil. For every one
> who does evil hates the light, and does not come to the light,
> lest his deeds should be exposed. But he who does what is true
> comes to the light, that it may be clearly seen that his deeds
> have been wrought in God. (3.17-21)

Faith changes and transfigures a person and fills him with spirituality, while disbelief leaves a person empty. Goethe once said that
faith is the mother of the miracle. Faith means to believe in a personal God who holds the world in His hands; it means to allow
Him to be God and Lord of all the facets and moments of your
life: to do miracles, to change you, to regenerate you, to save you.
It also means to live with God, to have Christ live in us instead of
ourselves.

What finally happened after the dialogue with Nicodemos, John
does not tell us. The purpose of the Evangelist is for us to understand little by little that Jesus is the Christ, the Savior, as John
himself had come to know him and as the Church had lived him.

In any case Nicodemos was not able to understand the mystery
of salvation, even though he was a teacher and had heard about
the preaching of John the Baptist (3.10-13).

The Second Testimony of the Baptist
John 3.22-36

After the dialogue with Nicodemos, John brings us to the
country, far from the noise of the city. The Baptist was still there
working—"for he had not yet been put into prison." Thus two
circles of disciples were formed—one around Jesus and the other
around John—and comparisons began to be made. The disciples
of the Baptist, however, began to be jealous and somehow complained to their teacher. At this point John the Baptist rose to the

height of a spiritual prophet and offered the highest testimony for the person of Christ:

> You yourselves bear me witness, that I said, I am not the Christ, but I have been sent before him. He who has the bride is the bridegroom; the friend of the bridegroom, who stands and hears him, rejoices greatly at the bridegroom's voice; therefore this joy of mine is now full. He must increase, but I must decrease.
>
> He who comes from above is above all; he who is of the earth belongs to the earth, and of the earth he speaks; he who comes from heaven is above all. He bears witness to what he has seen and heard, yet no one receives his testimony; he who receives his testimony sets his seal to this, that God is true. For he whom God has sent utters the words of God, for it is not by measure that he gives the Spirit; the Father loves the Son, and has given all things into his hand. He who believes in the Son has eternal life; he who does not obey the Son shall not see life, but the wrath of God rests upon him. (Jn.3.28-36).

The testimony is very sublime. And the manner by which John has preserved it is unique. Christ who came from above must increase in influence, while John must retreat. The light of the moon diminishes as the light of the sun rises. This was John's mission. "He was not the light, but came to bear witness to the light" (1.8).

The Dialogue With the Samaritan Woman.
The Messiah, the Living Water
John 4.1-42

The Pharisees began to suspect the movements of Christ and this time he left Judea. "His time had not yet come." Leaving for Galilee, Jesus passed through Samaria. "Jews have no dealings with Samaritans" (4.9). But this does not apply to Christ who came to unite all things into one with God.

The disciples went to purchase food, while Jesus remained behind at the well of Jacob and began a dialogue with the thirsty Samaritan woman. The dialogue ended with the subject of faith and true worship, which is the abiding question pertaining to the relationship between man and God (4.19-21).

To this thirsty woman Jesus revealed that he is the anticipated Messiah. He knows God and teaches us what He is and how we can worship Him properly.

You worship what you do not know; we worship what we know, for salvation is from the Jews. But the hour is coming, and now is, when the true worshippers will worship the Father in spirit and truth, for such the Father seeks to worship him. God is spirit, and those who worship him must worship in spirit and truth (4.22-24).

God is Spirit, unlimited by matter, by place and by time. He wants His worshipers to worship Him spiritually, with all of their being and in truth — realizing who God is, and what their relationship to Him is. These things, however, presuppose rebirth in spirit. The Spirit and Truth we have only in Christ and through Christ.

The words of Jesus were too deep and wishing to change the subject, she said: "We are waiting for the Messiah, He will explain these things to us. And Christ told her: "I who speak to you am he." It is remarkable that Jesus said this to the Samaritan woman and not to Nicodemos the teacher of Israel.

Christ revealed himself to this thirsty woman, that he is the coming Messiah. Did she understand him? Did she believe him? We cannot know exactly. She ran and called her fellow countrymen. And the Samaritans came, saw, believed and confessed, "This man really is the Savior of the world," the Christ.

These Samaritans were the first fruits of the endless harvest of the Gospel about which Christ spoke with his disciples in John 4. 31-38.

Christ left Samaria and the Gospel does not tell us anything else about the woman, just as it did not say anything more about what happened to Nicodemos. John is interested mainly in the testimonies for the person of Christ. The Church tells us that the Samaritan woman became Saint Fotini the missionary who was martyred for Christ together with her sisters and her children.

CHAPTER FOUR

THE GALILEAN MINISTRY

Jesus once again left for Galilee, possibly because the Pharisees seemed to be starting a movement against him (Jn.4.1-3). It is difficult for us to know if this coming into Galilee coincided with his ministry there as described in the Synoptic Gospels. In any case, we shall now leave for a while the Gospel of St. John to follow the Synoptic accounts of the Galilean ministry.

The Gospel of the Kingdom
Mark 1.13-15; Matthew 4.12-17

Now after John was arrested, Jesus came into Galilee, preaching the gospel of God, and saying, 'The time is fulfilled, and the kingdom of God is at hand; repent, and believe in the gospel.'

The Baptist had been imprisoned by King Herod and his voice had been silenced. The public ministry of Christ now became more systematic. His kerygma, his proclamation, was the *evangelion*, the good news of God to the world that the kingdom of God is near.

The kingdom of God means the condition of human life where all things are done in harmony with the holy will of God. It was for this purpose precisely that man was created and placed in paradise. This was the life in paradise. But this harmony of life was destroyed by man's sin, and life became a constant struggle. The hope of Israel and of all mankind was for a restoration of this life in the person of the Messiah.

It was in such an atmosphere that the first kerygma of Christ was heard. The time has been fulfilled; the time determined by

God has come and the kingdom of God is near, very soon it will become a reality. "Repent and believe this good news!"

For the kingdom of God to become a reality, it is necessary for man to cooperate with God! It is necessary for man to repent, to change radically his way of thinking, to turn toward God with all of his heart; to be in his proper relationship with God. This is what Christ came to tell us and to instill in our hearts. This is salvation, redemption, justification, life eternal, entrance into the kingdom of God.

The kingdom of God was the first proclamation of Christ, and it is this kingdom which He preached all His life. In the parables He spoke about the kingdom of God, and with the miracles He wanted us to see the kingdom of God realized in His person. The kingdom of God was the proclamation of the Apostles and this is the message of the Church of Christ. We begin our worship with the words: "Blessed is the Kingdom," and our constant prayer is "Thy Kingdom come." Everything else in the life of the Church is a derivative and a result of our faith and experience of the kingdom of God.

Let us now move on in the garden of Holy Scripture to see what more it tells us about the kingdom of God in words and deeds. Here we must remember that the Evangelists give us only signs, some notes from the words of Jesus. They presuppose many things from the oral tradition of the earliest Church. We have to formulate our opinion about the kingdom of God and the position which Christ holds in it by constantly going through the entire Holy Scriptures and the life of the Church. The Gospels grew out of the faith and life of the Church.

The Calling of the First Disciples
Mark 1.16-20; Matthew 4.18-25

Christ deliberately called the first disciples to constitute the nucleus of the kingdom of God. They would be the ones to continue His work after the Cross and the Resurrection. Epigrammatically the Evangelists describe how Jesus called the first disciples and how His imposing personality prevailed over them.

And Jesus said to them, "Follow me, and I will make you become fishers of men." And immediately they left their nets and followed him.

Later the circle of the twelve disciples was completed (Mk.3. 13). With the gathering of the disciples, the Gospel of the kingdom of God was continued. Even the miracles came as divine signs to testify on behalf of the person who proclaimed the kingdom. The miracles were mainly related to the psychic and spiritual healing of people. The kingdom of God is not a magically miraculous help from God for our daily needs, but rather a spiritual strengthening to easily overcome the needs and the problems of life.

The principle sign which revealed the divinity of Christ was His being recognized as the Son of God by the evil spirits whose work He had come to destroy. One such miracle of Christ is described very briefly but impressively in Mark 1.21-28. Here the evil spirit or demon recognized that Jesus of Nazareth was the Holy One of God, the Messiah. But the work of the Messiah is to destroy the work of Satan and to inaugurate the kingdom of God. Consequently, Jesus drove out the evil spirit and the sick man was healed.

The people were amazed and confessed that in the person of Christ, in His teaching and in His deeds there was something new. "What is this? A new teaching—and with authority! He even gives orders to evil spirits and they obey him!"

The news of Jesus spread quickly in all of Galilee and a new spiritual movement began everywhere. The people marveled, believed, and ran after Jesus, shouting that in His person "a great prophet has arisen among us...God has visited his people" (Lk.7. 16).

The Sermon on the Mount
Matthew 5.1-7,27

The Evangelists tell us generally that Jesus went throughout Galilee, teaching and preaching the good news of the kingdom. But they do not tell us what exactly He preached in those days. At this point Matthew gives us in some systematic order the most important points in the teaching of Christ which obviously were taught at different places and times during the three year period of His ministry. Because Christ used to preach on a hill near Capernaum, this entire section of teaching material assumed the heading "the Sermon on the Mount."

The Beatitudes
5.3-16

The first section of this exceptional collection contains the beatitudes. The beatitudes depict the extraordinary characteristics of the new life of those who are called to become members of the kingdom of God. The first characteristic is "poverty of spirit." Each believer needs to acknowledge his or her imperfection, to be contrite about it, to be humble before God, and to thirst for divine justice. Believers must be peaceful persons, and above all must have love and be merciful. Only such people can inherit the kingdom of God, become the true sons of God, see the glory of God.

The world can misunderstand Christians and indeed both Christ and Christians were persecuted in different ways. The Christians, however, will finally remain steadfast in their life and will enjoy the blessings of God in His kingdom; this is "the great reward in heaven." To this blessed group can belong people of all classes, even the tax collectors and the prostitutes who repented, believed and lived a godly life.

The second section of the Sermon on the Mount (Mt.5.17-7.23) contains a survey of the spiritual life at the time of Christ. In contrast to the letter of the Mosaic Law and the pharisaic traditions, Jesus emphasized the refinement and the depth which must characterize the new life in Christ. Christian virtue must be positive, not simply negative, prohibitive commandments. All the actions of the Christian must be done out of love for God and our fellow human beings—a love that embraces indiscriminately even enemies. Thus people become truly children of God, perfect, merciful as our heavenly Father (Lk.6.27-30). Greater honor than this cannot be given to man.

The Sermon on the Mount, on which we will speak again, is concluded by Matthew with the remark: "the crowds were astonished at his teaching, because he taught as one who had authority, and not as their scribes" (7.28-29). The people could see that Jesus was different. He spoke differently, with authority, as one who knows who he is and what his subject and his mission is. The people, however, did not yet recognize Jesus as they should; the divine requires experienced eyes to envision it as it reveals itself beneath human cover.

The Miracles Bear Witness to Christ
Matthew 8.1-27

After the Sermon on the Mount, Matthew again presents Jesus doing miracles. He heals the lepers, the servant of the centurion and many others. Matthew notes that these things were done to fulfill the prophecy of Isaiah about the Messiah: "He took our infirmities and bore our diseases" (Is.53.4; Mt.8.17).

Jesus rules over nature (Mt.8.27-34). In another incident Jesus calms the storm and some faith begins to appear among the people who begin to ask: "What sort of man is this that even the winds and sea obey him?" (Mt.8.27).

Two persons who were possessed by demons were cured in the country of the Gadarenes. The demons confessed that Jesus is the Son of God. The inhabitants of that country, however, did not understand the true meaning of the miracle, and they asked Jesus to leave from their country (8.28-34).

Jesus Forgives Sins
Matthew 9.1-8; Mark 2.1-12

The healing of the paralytic man is more instructive on the divinity of Christ. Instead of placing His hand on the paralytic and healing him, Jesus said: "Take heart, son; your sins are forgiven." The fanatic Pharisees were scandalized. "Who can forgive sins except God?" They considered Jesus' word as blasphemous because He assumed the prerogative of God and forgave sins. And it is with this accusation that later they were to lead Jesus to the Cross (Mk. 24.63).

At that point Jesus indicatively commanded the paralytic to get up. And indeed the sick man picked up his bed and walked away. People accused Jesus of considering Himself God. Jesus accepted this accusation and with the miracle of healing He showed that He is indeed the Messiah, the Son of man, and can heal the body and the soul. He can forgive sins on earth, in this present life. And it is here in this present life that sins must be forgiven, not in the final great judgment. Then it will be too late. This is the central teaching of the Church: in Christ our sins are forgiven, if we only repent and believe in Him.

Many times the sins and the mistakes in our life become the cause of illnesses. Medical science today knows that many illnesses are caused by psychological traumas. The love of Christ which forgives sins heals also the illness of the body. "A miracle is the restoration of nature to its perfect state of existence before the fall." Christ restored in man the "image of God" which had been distorted by the fall of man.

Responding to this miracle the people stood in awe and glorified God saying: "We never saw anything like this!" (Mk.2.12). Indeed the presence of Christ is something without comparison in history.

The Calling of Matthew the Tax Collector
Matthew 9.9-13

The calling of Matthew the tax collector is also a great miracle. With a single invitation from Jesus, Matthew left everything and "followed him." He became a disciple, an apostle who wrote for us the Gospel bearing his name. The conversion of Matthew and later of Zachaeus demonstrates for us the moral and spiritual influence which was exerted by the person of Christ upon people. Matthew will always be an example of how people should follow Christ: "And he left everything and rose and followed him" (Lk. 5.28). He made up his mind immediately and followed Jesus.

He Came to Call Sinners

Matthew, out of gratitude toward Jesus, prepared a dinner for Him. "While Jesus was having dinner at Matthew's house, many tax collectors and 'sinners' came and ate with Him and His disciples." The setting of this dinner is most revealing in highlighting the difference between the Gospel and the abundant love of Christ which embraces all persons and the restrictive spirit of the Law which keeps people at a distance from God. The liturgical rites are good, but it is necessary that they be natural expressions of love for God and our fellow men. Religion is respect and love for God and this love for God can be seen in the love we have for our fellow man, whoever he or she might be. His love, however, must always lead one toward the good, toward His salvation.

The Pharisees once again murmured and Jesus answered them: "Those who are well have no need of a physician, but those who are sick…'I desire mercy, and not sacrifice.' For I came not to call the righteous, but sinners" (Mt.9.12-13). In this verse Christ gives us the whole meaning of the Mystery of the Incarnation. No one is righteous, in the full sense of the word, before the Holy God. With repentance and faith, however, we can all be saved by God's mercy. This is precisely the reason, after all, why the Son of God came into the world—to seek the "lost sheep" and to bring us, through repentance and faith, to the Love of God. "Repent!" That is precisely the first proclamation.

At this point we must omit certain material from the Gospel according to Matthew for the sake of brevity: How one follows Christ (8.12-22); how we fast (9.14-17); the miracles of Jairus' daughter and the hemorrhaging woman (9.12-27). We select certain sections only from the garden of Holy Scripture. Mark omits more material and John even more. And yet in their own way they together give us a perfect image of the Person of Christ.

We only note here that the opposition of the "conservatives" against Jesus has begun. The blind and the possessed by demons acknowledge Him as the Son of David, as the Messiah. The so-called pious say that "He casts out demons by the prince of demons" (Mt. 9.34). Thus we come to another historical event in the life of Jesus.

The Testimony of Jesus for John the Baptist
Matthew 11.2-15

John the Baptist was still in prison. He had heard about the work of Christ. He saw, however, that the Messianic Kingdom had not yet been realized. His hope was to see it in his own time. He, too, expected the Messiah to come in power, to take up the shovel and the ax and to clean up the whole decadent condition. Unfortunately, this is exactly how all of us want the Messiah. He, however, chose to come in order to serve and to offer His life as a ransom for all. John, therefore, in his desire to know for sure, sent two of his disciples to ask Jesus: "Are you the one who was to come, or should we expect someone else?" Jesus did not answer directly and clearly, nor did He ever during His earthly life. He did answer indirectly. He apparently did certain miracles before the messengers who had come from John and then told them:

'...the blind receive their sight and the lame walk, lepers are cleansed and the deaf hear, and the dead are raised up, and the poor have good news preached to them. And blessed is he who takes no offense at me.' (Mt.11.4-6; Lk.7.21-25).

Such miracles were the traditional blessings expected from the Messiah and consequently served as silent testimonies to the fact that Jesus was indeed the expected Messiah, even if His kingdom had not yet openly prevailed. "The kingdom of God does not come visibly," with external power; it is a kingdom of the spirit, of the heart. People cannot say "'Lo, it is,' or 'There!' for behold, the kingdom of God is in the midst of you" (Lk.17.20-21).

When the messengers left, Jesus gave the highest testimony for John the Baptist: "Among those born of women there has not risen anyone greater than John the Baptist." John is the greatest prophet because God chose him to be the Forerunner who would introduce the Christ to the world. He is indeed the "Elijah" who was expected to prepare the people to accept the Messiah (Malachi 4.5). With this testimony for John, Jesus also bore testimony for Himself. If John is the forerunner for the Messiah, then Jesus is that Messiah, precisely because it was about Jesus that John testified. Jesus then *is* the expected Messiah and in His Person the messianic kingdom has been inaugurated and the faithful can seize it and enjoy its blessings. The faithful who have already received the kingdom can be considered greater than John the Baptist who at that moment was still expecting the kingdom to come.

It is clear from this section that Jesus is asking the people to believe that He is the expected Messiah-Savior. Seeing at that moment the disbelief of the many, Jesus derided the people who did not believe John nor Christ about whom John preached (Mt.11.16-24). And Jesus thanked God the Father who in His inscrutable will reveals the Mystery of Christ to those who are like little children with simple and open hearts.

CHAPTER FIVE

JESUS ENCOUNTERS OPPOSITION

The Sabbath Rest and Christ

The Pharisees not only did not believe, but they also followed Him everywhere with suspicion, seeking some opportune moment to accuse Him, even to destroy Him (Mt. 12.14). One thing that they readily found to accuse Him of was the breaking of the Sabbath rest by doing miracles on that day. This was considered a disobedience to the Mosaic Law. In a series of miracles in the Gospels, we can see the narrowness of the letter of the Law and the depth of the Spirit of Christ; the narrowness of the heart of the Pharisees and the breadth of the love of Christ who embraces all. Always responding to the comments of the Pharisees, Christ "put them to shame," thus showing the deeper spirit of the Law which is love.

In one instance when the disciples were hungry, they gleaned the wheat stalks and ate the kernels on a Sabbath. The Pharisees were scandalized by this and Jesus told them about David: If David ate out of necessity the holy bread in the sanctuary, and if the priests necessarily do some work on the Sabbath and you do not criticize them, then even more so you should not criticize my disciples. Here in my Person and in my work there is something greater than David and the sanctuary. The Law says, "I desire mercy, not sacrifice." "The Sabbath was made for man and not man for the Sabbath." Moreover, "the Son of Man (the Messiah) is Lord of the Sabbath (cf.Mt.12.1-8. Mk.2.23-28).

In the instance of other accusations, Jesus said that if we take

care of our animals when they are in danger and water them when
they are thirsty even on the Sabbath day, how much more should
we hasten to help our fellow man on the Sabbath. The Sabbath is
a good institution; it has been given to be a service to man, not to
enslave man. The deeper meaning of the Sabbath is not how to
avoid every possible activity, but rather how to use it for good
purposes, beneficial to ourselves and to our fellow man. In an instance where need will appear before us on the Sabbath day, our
question should be *what* shall we do: "to do good or to do harm,
to save life or to destroy?" (Lk.6.9). To simply avoid a particular
action does not benefit anyone; it is negative, useless and sometimes harmful for man (Mt.12.9-12. Lk.6.6-11, 13.10-17). We can
sometimes deny the letter of the Sabbath rest, but we can never
deny the spirit of the Law which is the worship of God and the
love of our neighbor. This is what God requires from man on the
Sabbath—the cultivation of love which is so necessary in the
life of the whole world. And this cultivation cannot be acheived
better than in our common worship as children of the one God-
Father.

With this sharp criticism from Jesus, the Pharisees' hatred in-
creased. They began to think of ways to get rid of Him. Thus the
Cross begins to be visible on the horizon.

Christ left, but the people followed Him and He advised them
not to reveal Him as Messiah anymore. Matthew notes at this point
that the Messiah was peaceful and avoided controversy just as
Isaiah had foreseen (Mt.12.15-21. Is.42.1-4).

The Unforgivable Sin
Matthew 12.22-37

The hatred of the Pharisees appeared even greater at the healing of a blind and deaf person. Observers had come now even from
Jerusalem. Jerusalem always had the last word. The miracle of
healing was obvious; they could not deny it. The people were
amazed and believed that Jesus must be the Messiah, "the Son of

David." The Pharisees slandered Jesus by saying, "it is only by Beelzebub, the prince of demons, that this man casts out demons" (Mt.12.24). Even Beelzebub himself could not think of such an accusation! Their evil had reached the limits of blasphemy—they denied God Himself, and Jesus did not pernit them such license. First He proved to them that common sense tells that it is impossible for Satan to drive out Satan because this would be his destruction. This should prove that Jesus drives out demons by the "Spirit of God." God is present and works in Christ. This again means that Christ is the stronger one who can drive out Satan. Thus the miracle as a whole also testifies that in Christ "the kingdom of God has come" upon us (Mt.12.28). "The reason the Son of God appeared was to destroy the devil's work."

After overturning their accusations, Jesus indicted the Pharisees for having become, with their evil manner, guilty of the greatest, the unforgivable sin. "Therefore I tell you, every sin and blasphemy against the Spirit will not be forgiven . . . either in this age or in the age to come" (Mt. 12.31-32). About Christ and His work one could possibly say something and be forgiven. But for one to deny by word and deed the presence and energy of the Holy Spirit of God in the work of Christ—this is precisely the unforgivable sin. The person who egotistically denies the presence of the Holy Spirit denies God himself, the God of love, and recognizes Satan as the only ruler of the world. For man to take such a position over and against God means that he has become completely saturated by evil and there is no hope of repentance and salvation. This is the main sin of the Pharisees and of every person who stubbornly denies the presence of the divine in Christ. This is why Christ admonished us to be careful in our words, in our thoughts and in our actions. "For by your words you will be justified, and by your words you will be condemned" (Mt.12.37). Our words are the overflow of the heart—either for good or for evil, and God is mainly concerned about our hearts.

Need for Repentance and Faith

Whatever Christ said he said out of love for us to call us to repentance and faith, as becomes clear in the following text (Mt.12. 38-42).The Pharisees have realized that Jesus challenged them to believe that he is the Messiah, and they asked him to show them a sign in order to believe. They had been accustomed to the many signs which God had shown in history for his people. The entire history of the Israelites, one can say, is a history of the signs of God (1 Cor.1.22. Jn.6.30). Christ, however, gave only one sign, "the sign of Jonah." Jonah is a *type* for the Resurrection of Christ on the third day, but primarily he is a sign of repentance unto salvation. The Ninevites heard Jonah's message, repented and were saved. Here now we have one who is greater than Jonah and greater than Solomon; we have the Messiah who came to call people to repentance; to forgive and to save the world.

Repentance was the very first message of Christ. Repentance will also be the final message (Lk.24.47). Repentance and forgiveness are the greatest gifts of religion to man struggling in life. Many times in life man takes the wrong road and gets lost. When repentance is genuine, it brings him back to life, to God. It is never too late for repentance. The Pharisees, however, were not yet ready for repentance; they remained unrepentant, and many people today, driven by false ego, remain unrepentant.

Who Are the Brothers of Christ
Matthew 12.46-50

On one occasion when Jesus was speaking to the people his mother and his brothers came to him. According to the tradition of the Church, the brothers of Jesus are either children of Joseph from a previous marriage (before he was engaged to Mary), or they are another kind of relative which could be called brother according to Jewish social customs. Jesus seized the opportunity of his relatives' presence to speak about the deeper meaning of spiritual relationships: "For whoever does the will of my Father in heaven is my brother, and sister, and mother" (Mt.12.50). All the faithful are one holy family.

CHAPTER SIX

THE PARABLES

The Parables

At this point Matthew presents a series of .the parables of the Lord. Many prophets and teachers used to teach with parables and the Jewish people were accustomed to this manner of teaching.

The parable, sometimes short and sometimes longer, is an image properly drawn from everyday life who'se purpose is to teach by analogy a certain moral or religious truth. The world of nature as we know it in our daily life can easily guide us, if we observe it carefully, to the spiritual, the divine and invisible realities of life. This is how Jesus and Paul and all great men and women observe the world of nature and of life. The parable is a lesson conveyed through an image taken from life (e.g. sowing, harvesting, marriage, commerce, construction, etc.) and thereby made more concrete and understandable. It captures the interest of the listener and helps him to comprehend the truth, to make it personal and to remember it easily as a source of inspiration in his life. The parable, however, requires good will—an eye that is willing to see and an ear that is willing to hear—in order for someone to grasp and receive the truth, the central message, which is often hidden in the parable. This is especially true when it comes to matters of faith, which is precisely the case with the parables of Jesus.

If we take the word parable (*para-vole*) literally we might believe that it seeks to somehow conceal the truth. Such an idea seems to be expressed in Mt. 13.13-15. This is why some people think that Jesus spoke in parables because he did not want the leaders who hated him to understand him. Christ, however, wants everyone to understand him and to be saved. The meaning of the text in Mt.

13.13-15 is rather understood in this manner: There are people who are not interested in the truth or the truth disturbs them by upsetting their egoism or their evil deeds in life and therefore they do not wish to see the truth. They become willingly blind, closing their eyes to the light of truth as if afraid to see, to hear and perhaps to repent and be saved! Those who thirst for the truth, however, and approach Christ with love can easily enter into the mystery of truth and together with faith and personal effort progress in knowledge and become perfect. This is what Jesus meant when he said: "To you it has been given to know the secrets of the kingdom of heaven" (Mt.13.11). It depends on each person how he or she will understand a parable and how he or she will benefit from it (cf.13.51-52).

With the parables Jesus wants to teach the nature of the coming kingdom, which is the subject of all Christian teaching. Each parable refers to some aspect of the kingdom of God: what is the kingdom; how does it develop until it fills the whole world; how must we receive it?

The Parable of the Sower
Matthew 13.1-23

A careful study of this parable will reveal several points. First, it reveals that its theme, as is true of all the parables, is the mysteries of the kingdom of God: how we may enter the kingdom of God and how we may become the beloved and elect people of God. Second, it shows that the kingdom of God is won with the "word," which, like seed, is sown, grows and bears fruit. This means that the kingdom of God is present, even if it is only a seedling. Also present is the king who sows the "word." The word has become flesh and is now walking among us. Third, the kingdom of God is a gift of God for everyone. The word of the kingdom is sown everywhere and all are invited to receive it. The success of the sowing, however, depends on the quality of the earth, that is, us. We are free spiritual beings and each one of us has to offer something in order to receive the kingdom of God. That something is our heart. The more we give our heart to Christ, the more we permit him to cultivate it and the more certain is our success. The image of the parable tells us that three-fourths of the seed is lost. The people do not receive the word, they do not give their hearts abundantly to Christ. They allow their hearts to remain a prisoner of the world and its pleasures, so that they cannot bear fruit. One part, however, that which receives the word in "a good and virtuous heart," bears the fruit of faith and virtue – thirty, sixty and even one hundred times what was sown. The conclusion is that despite the apparent failure of the word, the harvest will actually be abundant, the work of the Gospel will bring its fruits. The "house of God" will be filled, as it is noted elsewhere, and the kingdom of God will be realized "on earth as it is in heaven." The Church prays to God for workers to sow the word of God's kingdom and for hearts to receive that word with faith and love and to gather "fruit for eternal life, so that the sower and the reaper may rejoice together" (Jn.4.36).

The Parable of the Weeds
Matthew 13.24-30

In another parable again, Jesus taught how in the field of the Church there will grow among the wheat weeds also. But the harvest will come, the end and the judgment. Then God, who alone knows everthing, will separate the weeds from the wheat. The harvest symbolizes the end of the world with a double meaning: For the faithful the end will be a harvest of the crops, an entrance into the kingdom of God and eternal life. On the other hand, the end will be a judgment and eternal suffering for those who have not believed. The same lesson is taught by the parable of the fishing nets (Mt.13.47-50).

Some Other Parables

The parables of the mustard seed and of the leaven again show the dynamic force which the kingdom of God has. By wordly standards it appears to have small and insignificant beginnings – the Apostles were the first small flock but in time it grows and with God's help reaches its goal without us realizing just how it happened. The small seed becomes a great tree. The small amount of yeast, as a spiritual force, transforms the world. The seed of wheat ripens for harvest. The Church of Christ will spread and be established throughout the world (Mt.13.31-33. Mk.4.26-32).

CHAPTER SEVEN

JESUS THE SON OF GOD

A precise and complete history of the life of Jesus was neither attempted by the Apostles nor reconstructed by theologians. The purpose of the Gospel is not historical curiosity but the person of Christ and the kingdom of God he came to bring to us. We have already noted previously in this book that Jesus had been recognized by many as the Messiah-Christ, but he had also experienced the hatred of the leaders because he presumably did not honor the Sabbath. These facts are presupposed in Jn.5.9-16. For this reason we can more easily place here the material included in John 5 and, taking a brief recess from his life in Galilee, we can follow Jesus while he is in Jerusalem.

"After this there was a feast of the Jews, and Jesus went up to Jerusalem" (Jn.5.). This feast of Purim was celebrated about one month before the Passover and probably Jesus thought of staying there until the Passover to speak to the people about the kingdom of God.

The Healing of the Paralytic
John 5.1-15

Of the many miracles which Jesus probably did at this time, John picks one out — the healing of the paralytic — to show us Christ bearing the infirmities of the world. The brief dialogue between Christ the Savior and the suffering paralytic is dynamic. Christ saw the human pain and asked: "Do you want to get well?" The question is strange. Who does not want to get well? The inva-

lid replied: "Sir, I have no one to help me into the pool when the
water is stirred." Inspired by this text, a hymn writer of our
Church has Jesus speak poetically to the invalid.

It is for you that I became man and you say you have no one?
Pick up your bed and walk!

The paralytic was cured; he picked up his bed and walked away.
And John notes: "The day on which this took place was a Sabbath." The Pharisees consequently again complained and sought to
persecute Jesus for "doing these things on the Sabbath."

The Son of God, the Judge, the Son of Man
John 5.17-30

The paralytic was healed and the Pharisees were grumbling. The
conflict between them and Jesus was becoming extremely taut. In
response to the comments of the Jews, Jesus took the opportunity
to give the highest testimony for the Father and for himself (17-
29).

"My Father is working still, and I am working." ... the Son can
do nothing of his own accord, but only what he sees the Father
doing; for whatever he does, that the Son does likewise... For as
the Father raises the dead and gives them life, so also the Son
gives life to whom he will (Jn.5.17,19,21).

With the clear self-awareness that He is the expected Messiah —
the Son of God — Jesus responds authoritatively: "My Father is
working still, and I am working" (Jn.5.17). By these words Jesus
separated himself from the other people: He made God his own
Father and himself equal to God. For this reason the Jewish leaders sought to kill him (Jn.5.16,18). But Jesus responded: the Son
does whatever he sees the Father doing. The work of the Father
and the Son is one and the same and it is the endless work of creation and salvation of the world which has no "Sabbath," that is,
no rest. The Church sees the "blessed Sabbath" for Christ after he
finished his work on the cross, and rested in the tomb.

The particular work of the Father is *to give life* but also *to
judge the world.* Both of these works have been given to the Son
also. The Father gives life and judges the world *through the Son,*
so "that all may honor the Son, even as they honor the Father"

(Jn.5.23). The Son judges because he is the "Son of Man," the anticipated Messiah-Judge (Daniel 7.13-14).

The Son Raises the Dead (Jn.5.24-29)

Faith in the words of Jesus gives life, while disbelief brings spiritual death. Spiritual death is separation from God not only in this life but also in the day of the general resurrection "when all who are in the tombs will hear his voice and come forth, those who have done good, to the resurrection of life, and those who have done evil, to the resurrection of judgement" (Jn.5.28-29).

In order to be raised up at the parousia of Christ and to have eternal life, we must first be raised up here spiritually through faith in the person and the words of Christ (5.24-25). It is necessary for us here and now to "live a new life" (Rom.6.3-6).

Jesus closes dogmatically this section of self-testimony: "I can do nothing on my own authority; as I hear, I judge; and my judgement is just, because I seek not my own will but the will of him who sent me." (5.30). The words of Jesus about life and judgment are true because they are words he hears from the Father,"I am in the Father" (1.18,14.10).

Who Witnesses to Christ?

With these words Jesus challenged the Jews to believe. But they did not seem to be ready to believe. Perhaps they were looking for more proofs. And Jesus added more proofs about himself and thereby made them more responsible (5.31-45). The only witness who could, humanly speaking, testify for Jesus was John the Baptist, and he testified (1.29,36;3.28-36). But the testimony of John was limited; he was a mere lamp before the Light which is Christ. The value of John's testimony was in that he heard the voice of God and saw the Holy Spirit coming upon Jesus at his baptism. The greater and weightier testimony, however, was that of the Father. Only the Father can really testify about Christ the *Theanthropos* (Mt.11.27). Without divine inspiration Christ cannot be known (1.Cor. 12.3).

"For the works which the Father has granted me to accomplish, these very works which I am doing, bear me witness that the Father has sent me" (Jn.5.36). The testimony of the Father for the Son became known first of all in the work of salvation which Jesus was now doing and the miracles accompanying it testified as impartial witnesses that Jesus was indeed the Savior sent by God (10. 25,38;14.11;17.4;19.28).

The Father has testified for Jesus personally in sacred Scripture. The main purpose of Scripture, of Moses and of all the Prophets is one: to point to, to look toward the coming Messiah sent by God. So Jesus continued to accuse the Jewish leaders who presumably knew the Scriptures: It seems that you have not heard his voice nor have you seen his face. You have not accepted his word deeply in your hearts. This is demonstrated by the fact that you did not accept me as the one about whom the Father spoke in the Scriptures (5.37-38). You scrutinize the Scriptures but only scholastically and superficially, and therefore do not understand their real message about Christ who is the source of life (5.39-40). You have preserved the dead letter but lost the spirit of life.

And Jesus continues: I do not say these things because I am seeking glory from you. Glory from men I neither seek nor need. It is my Father who glorifies me" (Jn.8.54). I am simply telling you the truth and the truth is that you do not believe me and that you do not love Moses nor God nor me whom he has sent. Moses himself about whom you boast will judge you for your unbelief. Since you do not believe in Moses, who is your hope and your admiration, how can you ever believe my words?

In this chapter of John we see in compact form all of the faith of the Church about Jesus Christ. The testimony began as a dialogue and developed into a sublime monologue. Man's relationship to God is indeed a real dialogue. But when God begins to speak, we then have essentially, a monologue through which God reveals himself to man. Man is present but his role is mainly to listen, to learn. Only after a person has listened and has learned can he speak freely, conscientiously and responsibly and say "yes" and "Amen." This is the best way we can participate in the divine dialogue of a prayer or a meditation. No one can every say "no" to God. If a person does not say the "Amen," the dialogue remains a monologue; man receives nothing and remains empty, alone, as he was before the dialogue began with God—the dialogue which he so much needs in life.

In this dialogue-monologue, as John has preserved it for us, Christ is presented as one with the Father. For one to believe and to honor God he must believe and honor the Son (5.23). For "no one comes to the Father, except by me...He who has seen me has seen the Father." (Jn.14.6,9). We can see the Father and listen to the Father only in Christ who became man for us. All of Christology of the Church is expressed in those phrases of John . This, however, must be a personal experience in our lives. John has deeply experienced Christ in his life and therefore he could describe so well Christ as being one with the Father. Without this experience of the presence and energy of God in us, we have not yet reached that faith which saves. This is why faith needs constant examination to determine how deeply we actually live the mystery of Christ.

The words which Christ said were an invitation to faith. He expected a "yes" and an "Amen." The Jewish leaders do not seem to have replied. The atmosphere was not conducive, and actually became more hostile (7.1). The chapter ends abruptly because of this hostile atmosphere. Christ again left for Galilee. He did not remain in Jerusalem for the Passover Feast (6.1-4). At the very next Passover Feast Jesus was to be upon the Cross for us.

CHAPTER EIGHT

JESUS RETURNS TO GALILEE

John with a simple "after this" leads us directly "to the far shore of the Sea of Galilee," where the feeding of the 5,000 persons took place. John did not want to write much about Jesus' activities in Galilee. The Synoptics have written enough about them. Here again John selects just one miracle and around this miracle gives us all of the teaching of Christ in Galilee with its results, which are the same as those in the Synoptics.

Because of this we can here leave John for a moment to return to the Synoptics, particularly at the point where Jesus sends his twelve disciples to do missionary work.

The Sending of the Twelve Disciples
Mark 6.7-13

Jesus apparently sent more than once his disciples to do missionary work in the towns of Galilee (cf. a) Mt.9.35-10, Mk.3.13-19; b) Mk.6.7-13, Lk.9.1-6; c) Lk.10.1-16). We shall take here, for our basis, the second commission.

Jesus traveled throughout all the towns of Galilee and saw that the people of God had been left without good shepherds. The spiritual harvest was great and good workers were always scarce. Therefore, Jesus called the twelve disciples, endowed them with power and sent them to the various towns to preach the Good News of God's kingdom. Luke notes that Jesus spent the night in prayer before sending his disciples (6.12-13). Later, he also tells us of another commision of seventy disciples (10.1-24).

The Evangelists describe in detail the directions which Jesus gave to his disciples for the success of their mission. (Some of these, particularly about persecutions, could have been given later when the hatred of the Jews became more open). Absolute simplicity must characterize the apostle of the Good News of Christ. But alas to those who do not receive them. "For he who rejects me rejects him who sent me." (Mk.6.8-11; Lk.10.1-16). Thus, the disciples preached everywhere, calling the people to repentence. "And they cast out many demons, and anointed with oil many that were sick and healed them" (Mk.6.13).

The fame of Christ reached everywhere in Galilee. It reached also King Herod Antipas, who had previously beheaded John the Baptist (Mt.13.10; Mk.6.16,27; Lk.9.9), and who now was fearful that in the person of Jesus, John had come back to life (Mk.6.14-19; Mt.14.1-13).

The Return of the Twelve from the Mission
(Mk.6.30; Lk.10.17-27)

Here we shall take Luke as our basis because his account is more descriptive (even though it appears that his words have been said of a later time). The disciples returned with great joy. Even the demons had been defeated by faith in the name of the Jesus Christ. In this strong faith and great joy of the disciples, Christ saw the kingdom of God becoming a reality on earth. The Father has given the Son everything for the new economy of Salvation (Lk.10.22; Jn.5.22,17.2). With the power which faith in his name provides the believer can trample under foot "every power of the enemy" and nothing will ever harm them now (10.17-19). These are signs of the kingdom of God. Yet the joy of the disciples should not be based on the miracles which they can do through Christ. A joy based on the miracles could lead them to pride that destroys everything. The joy of the disciples should be primarily based on the fact that their names have been written in the books of the kingdom of heaven; they are the first members of the kingdom of God.

At this time the heart of Jesus was full of joy and he broke out into a thanksgiving for the faith of his disciples:

'I thank thee, Father, Lord of heaven and earth, that thou hast hidden these things from the wise and understanding and revealed them to babes; yea, Father, for such was thy gracious will.

All things have been delivered to me by my Father; and no one knows who the Son is except the Father, or who the Father is except the Son and any one to whom the Son chooses to reveal him' (10.21-22).

The phenomenon of faith has its roots in the real relationship which a person has with God. Man is created in the image of God and lives through his communion with God. God, in himself, is invisible and incomprehensible and man alone cannot find God who exceeds every human thought. Man can only thirst for God. In our thirst God condescends by virtue of divine economy and reveals himself to us in a variety of ways and calls us to faith. The most complete revelation was in Christ. In Christ God became man and in his human form we saw the glory of God. He who believes and receives Christ knows the Father also, "He who has seen me has seen the Father," Christ said (Jn.13.8-12,17.3). Even this faith in Christ is a gift of God. "No one can say, 'Jesus is Lord,' except by the Holy Spirit" (1 Cor.12.3). With the wisdom of this world one cannot come to know the mystery of the Father and the Son. God enlightens the "children," the pure hearts to know Christ (cf.Mt. 16.16).

Blessed are the eyes that can see Christ. All of the Prophets yearned to see him and did not (10.23-24).

Without revelation we cannot have the right faith about Christ. Let us then pray for God to reveal to us the Son and to keep our hearts open to know Christ and in Christ to know the Father, the Holy Trinity, as the Apostles and the Church know him.

The Feeding of the Five Thousand
Matthew 14.13-21; Mark 6.30-44; Luke 9.10-17; John 6.1-59

When Jesus heard of the death of John and the thoughts of Herod Antipas (Mt.13.1-2), he went away to a deserted place. The effort had been strenuous and it was necessary to rest both physically and spiritually (Mk.3.20-21,6.31-34). Jesus and his disciples hadn't even reached their destination for a rest when crowds of people were already forming there. Jesus had compassion on them, for they were like sheep without a shepherd and he began to teach them many things. The people were thirsty and the work was end-less—long hours of teaching and many miracles. As the time passed the disciples began to show concern for the crowds of people. They urged Jesus to let them go, to give them a brief recess to get something to eat. But the people should not be dismissed wanting; rather they should be filled. So Jesus said: "You give them some-thing to eat." And the disciples were overwhelmed; they had very little food and the crowd was great. How would it be possible? Christ then said to them: Bring whatever you have (bring whatever you have of faith, too!). Jesus blessed the five loaves of bread and the two fish, and gave them to the disciples and the disciples in turn passed them out to the people. "They ate and were satisfied" and there were even leftovers!

The scene was very impressive and John with his comments makes it even more powerful. It was the time of the Passover Feast, springtime with plenty of green grass. Jesus and his disciples should have been in Jerusalem. The incidents, however, recorded in the fifth chapter of John forced them to be far away in Galilee. Thus the feeding of the five thousand took the form of a Passover celebration.

How was the miracle done? Do not try to explain it. No matter what you say with your reason about the miracle, you will probab-ly detroy it. Leave it as the four Gospels have preserved it. Receive the miracle into you heart, and the whole scene, for this is its pur-pose: the revelation of the divine to the degree we can receive it. And where the divine is present everything is possible, even if it is beyond human reason. In this miraculous feeding of the people Jesus revealed himself as the anticipated Messiah already among his people teaching the truth and nourishing them both spiritually and physically. This was how the Jews of that time expected their Messiah. John notes that at this time the Galileans wanted to de-clare him king. Their faith in the Messiah was a faith for "food," for earthly goods. This was why Jesus left everyone, including his disciples, and went up into a mountain for prayer. The moments were critical and required communion with the Father. Without prayer and communion with the Father nothing worthwhile can be achieved in life.

Jesus Walks on the Water
Matthew 13.22-33; Mark 6.45-52

Christ, high up on the hill, was praying. Down below the disciples alone now in the sea of Galilee were having a rough time. Early in the morning "they saw Jesus approaching the boat, walking on water." The disciples were terrified. "But he said to them, 'It is I; do not be afraid'" (Jn. 6.20). His voice reassured them. Peter wanted to go out of the boat and meet him in the sea. But his faith was not yet strong enough and he began to sink. Christ reached out his hand and caught him."'You of little faith,' he said, 'why did you doubt?' . . . And those in the boat worshiped him, saying, 'Truly you are the Son of God'" (Mt. 14.31-33). The wind having calmed down, they crossed over to the other side of the lake and landed at Gennesaret (Mk.6.45-56, Jn.6.16-21).

The Signs and Faith in Christ

The divine is not revealed to man directly but through signs and in parables. God appears and acts before us in symbols and symbolic actions inviting us to understand these signs and to make a decision, to believe. The miracle-parable of the feeding of the five thousand people, together with the related teaching, was one of the most Messianic signs of Jesus. He expected the faith of the people. But unfortunately they did not show the correct faith. For this reason Jesus said to the people who came to see him in Capernaum:

'Truly, truly, I say to you, you seek me, not because you saw signs, but because you ate your fill of the loaves. Do not labor for the food which perishes, but for the food which endures to eternal life, which the Son of man will give to you; for on him has God the Father set his seal' (Jn. 6.26-27).

We often seek God only for our worldly and daily needs. We want *to be helped by him* rather than *to follow him*. Even Peter showed little faith and all the disciples confessed that they did not know him, "for they did not understand about the loaves, but their hearts were hardened" (Mk.6.52).

Jesus is the Bread of Life
John 6.28-58

The Galileans and especially the leaders realized that Jesus requires faith, but instead they only asked for more signs. Most sermons today deal with promises for signs and warnings of destruction in order to create in the people faith and obedience to Christ.

At another time Jesus had responded to such requests for signs with the sign of Jonah, the sign of repentance for salvation. In John, however, Jesus responds differently and gives the greatest testimony for his person and his work as the Savior of the world. The Jews sought for a sign, for bread from heaven—again their minds were on food. And Jesus responded clearly and steadfastly that he himself is the real sign from heaven. He is the heavenly bread who came from the Father and gives eternal life (Jn.6.25-58), not the manna which Moses offered in the desert.

'I am the bread of life; he who comes to me shall not hunger, and he who believes in me shall never thirst . . . For I have come down from heaven, not to do my own will, but the will of him who sent me...For this is the will of my Father, that every one who sees the Son and believes in him should have eternal life: and I will raise him up at the last day' (Jn.6.35-40).

The Jews were grumbling again. They could not believe. They saw Jesus as simply a man, the son of Joseph. For someone to really believe these things he must have a special calling and the guidance from the Father; he or she must be "taught by God." John knew this because he himself was taught by God through Christ and remembered the words well and recorded them with great care (Jn.6.40-46). All the Gospels emphasize that faith is something divine; it comes from God to those whose heart is open. At this point the first phase of the dialogue closes with an authoritative note: "Truly, truly I say to you, he who believes in me has eternal life" (Jn.6.47-50).

The Cross and the Eucharist
John 6.51-59

'I am the living bread which came down from heaven; if any one eats of this bread, he will live for ever; and the bread which I shall give for the life of the world is my flesh' (Jn.6.51).

Jesus became the bread of life at his death on the Cross. The faithful will "eat his flesh" and "drink his blood" and will have "eternal life" and Christ will raise them up at the last day. When John wrote these things he had in mind the Eucharist with which the Church lived. He knew that the "flesh" and the "blood" of the Eucharist was real food and drink unto eternal life. The Holy Eucharist is a real union with Christ and in this mystical union there is life.

'He who eats my flesh and drinks my blood abides in me and I in him. As the living Father sent me, and I live because of the Father, so he who eats me will live because of me' (Jn.6.56-57; 1 Cor.10.16-17).

Once again John concludes the subject emphatically: "This is the bread that came down from heaven . . . he who eats this bread will live forever (Jn.6.58). He said this while teaching in the synogogue in Capernaum (Jn.6.59). For John this was the entire teaching of Jesus in Galilee. In the synogogue the attitude of the Galileans toward Christ was judged. In John 6.60-71, we have a description of the results of Jesus' teaching: "This is a hard teaching. Who can listen to it?" "After this many of his disciples drew back and no longer went about with him" (Jn.6.60,66) the opposite of "believing and being his disciples."

Jesus then turned to the twelve Apostles and said: "Will you also go away?" The question was a difficult one at this critical hour, and Peter hastened to reply. "Lord, to whom shall we go? You have the words of eternal life. We believe and know that you are the Holy One of God," the Christ. Peter gave his confession for the twelve, yet one among them was Judas who would betray him and Christ knew it! The Synoptics, too, conclude here with the Confession of Peter.

The Things That Make a Person Unclean
Mark 7.1-23

Jesus saw that the results of his work in Galilee had been determined. The people did not believe. As John indicates, Jesus should have gone to Judea, but he remained in Galilee because in Judea they were seeking to kill him (cf.7.1f). In Galilee too Jesus was being watched. Some teachers of the Law had gone there from Jerusalem to spy on him and had found his fault: "his disciples eat food with unclean hands" (Mk.7.1-6)! Jesus responded to them and taught us, too, that true piety is primarily in the heart and not in dead formalities, particularly when the formalities are separated from their original meaning, from the will of God. That which comes out of the heart is what sanctifies or pollutes a person (Mk. 7.7-23,Mt.15.1-20). When our heart is empty of high ideals, then all things are polluted, even the higher expressions of faith. We can use even religion to humiliate rather than exhalt our neighbor. And this is a terrible thing.

In the Region of Tyre and Sidon

At this time Jesus traveled to the region of Tyre. His work was moving toward its conclusion and he wanted to be alone with his disciples. A Greek woman, a pagan from Canaan sought mercy and help for her daughter who was seriously ill. She called him "Lord, Son of David." The faith which Jesus did not find among the Jews he found in a "stranger." At another time he found it in a Samaritan or in a centurian. For her great faith Jesus healed the daughter of the Canaanite woman from a distance (Mk.7.31-8,26; Mt.15. 29-16.12).

The Confession of Peter
Mark 8.27-33; Matthew 16.13-23; Luke 9.18-22

After this Jesus traveled to the north section of Palestine, to the exceptionally beautiful region of Palestine, Caesarea Philippi. The time was a few months before the Cross and Jesus sought to approach even more the heart of his disciples. He wanted to help them to know him better. They were the ones who would continue his work and they would need to know him well and to confess clearly what they believed about his person. A faith that is not confessed is not yet clear and steadfast. At first Jesus put the question in general and neutral terms: "Who do people say I am?" or who do people say the Son of Man is? (meaning himself). The disciples enumerated the opinions which the people had about the person of Christ. Then Jesus asked them directly:*"But who do you say that I am?"*

The questions undoubtedly troubled the disciples during the time they were together, as it troubled all those who heard Jesus speak. From the teaching, the parables and the miracles of Christ the people would ask themselves: "Who is this man?" And the answer was given according to the personal character of each person. Some believed and some were scandalized because they knew his origin (Mk.6.2-6). Some called him a great prophet from God and others called him a deceiver of the people. The crowds were amazed by his teaching, a new teaching with authority and not like that of the teachers of the law (Mk.1.27,11.28). Still others approached the truth even closer. They believed that Jesus was Elijah or one of the prophets. That was how they expected some prophet to come in the last days to prepare the coming of the Messiah. Some people recognized Jesus as "Lord," "Son of David" (Mk.7. 28;Mt.22.41). They could not, however, express themselves clearly and in this they were hindered by the leaders.

All these things were said by the people in general. But what did Jesus have to say about himself? It is his own testimony about himself that is most important for our faith. His teaching and his miracles help us certainly to formulate some idea about the person of Christ. But it is from the personal testimony of Jesus that we can see more deeply the mystery of the person and work of Christ. Christ preached that the kingdom of God is not only near but already present in his person. John the Baptist used to say that "among you stands one who is stronger." Christ used to say that the kingdom of God has come upon you, while the kingdom of Satan is being abolished (Mt.12.24-30). The presence of Christ is something "greater" than Jonah, Solomon, the temple and even David. Jesus is the Messiah anticipated by the Patriarchs and the

Prophets. He is the "Son of Man" who will judge the world, who will forgive sins, who will give life to the world (Jn.5.17-30). After all of these and many other comments we can understand the weight carried by the personal question directed by Jesus to the disciples: "Who do you say I am?"

The question was personal and the disciples had to answer it personally and responsibly, just as everyone who comes into a personal relationship with Christ through the Gospel or in the life of the Church where he has been born has to answer it. Everyone who bears his holy name must answer this question personally and responsibly as a matter of life and death, as a personal relationship with Christ, and not simply as a literary or sociological matter. And it may be necessary to answer this question many times in our life. In the person of Christ we meet God and when God meets us, we cannot speak irresponsible and indefinitely. No one can give us a cut and dry answer for the person of Christ which is as convincing and satisfactory as the one we ourselves can and must give with God's help always.

In the case of the disciples, it was Peter who first gave the answer on behalf of all of them: "You are the Christ, the Son of the living God" (Mt.16.16). Peter, as we shall see later on, had not yet fully realized the whole truth of this confession. He understood the Messiah in the national, Israelite sense. This could easily be misunderstood by the people with disastrous results for the whole mission. Only after the Cross and the Resurrection would there be a full concept of the Messiah. This was the reason for the strict warning: "not to tell anyone that he was the Christ" (Mt.15.20; Mk:8.30; Lk.9.21).

In any case, this Confession, as the Church believes it and lives it, contains all the truth of the Christian faith. It confesses that Jesus from Nazareth is the expected Christ-Savior of the world, the eternal Son and Word of God, and God who became man to help us become "sons of God." Furthermore, it confesses that Jesus is the Lamb of God who bears the sins of the world. In his person the kingdom of God began upon earth and he reigns over his Church and in the whole world.

"Blessed are you, Simon Bar-Jona! For flesh and blood has not revealed to you, but my Father who is in heaven" (Mt.16.17). Jesus accepted the confession of Peter and assured him that this confession is not a human achievement but a revelation, a gift from God himself. Upon this revealed confession, Christ founded his Church. And indeed the Church was founded on this truth and remains forever. And as long as the confession of faith is strong and clear the powers of evil which have their citadel in Hades will never prevail against the Church.

Christ Must Suffer

From that time Jesus began to show his disciples that he must go to Jerusalem and suffer many things from the elders and chief priests and scribes, and be killed, and on the third day be raised. (Mt.16.21)

After the Confession of Peter Jesus began to reveal to his disciples who Christ really is: Jesus is Christ, king, but the reaching of full glory must be preceded by the Cross and the Resurrection.

As soon as Peter heard that the Messiah would have to suffer, he was scandalized and began to teach Jesus: "God forbid, Lord! This shall never happen to you": (Mt.16.23). The eternal and inscrutable will of God is to save the world through the Cross of Love and any one who goes against the will of God is Satan.

Here for the first time the true nature of the Messiah was revealed. The messiah is the Lamb of God who must suffer out of divine love for the salvation of his people (cf. Isaiah 53). A royal messiah with power and glory we can all easily accept. It was such a messiah that Peter had in mind. A Christ who goes toward the Cross with no worldly opposition can only with great difficulty be accepted by man. The Cross was and will be foolishness and a stumbling block for the many. For those who believe, however, the Crucified Christ is "the power of God and the wisdom of God" for salvation. That is how St. Paul and the Church knew and preached the Mystery of Christ. The Gospel was and is the Gospel of the Crucified Christ (1 Cor. 1.18-25, Acts 17.3).

'If any man would come after me, let him deny himself and take his cross, and follow me. For whoever would save his life will lose it; and whoever loses his life for my sake and the gospel's will save it. For what does it profit a man, to gain the whole world and forfeit his life? For what can a man give in return for his life?' (Mk.8.34-37)

At this point the high teaching about the sacrificial character of the new life in Christ was revealed. The life of man is won with the love which is ready to be sacrificed for the common good, for the will of God. This is precisely how we saw it in the life of Jesus Christ.

The Transfiguration
Matthew 17.1-8; Mark 9.2-8; Luke 9.28-36

From the day of Peter's Confession, Christ saw the Cross approaching closer and closer. His spirit was turned toward Jerusalem. It is there that his work would be judged. From time to time he would mention the Passion as a sort of preparation. It is as one such preparation that we may understand the marvelous Transfiguration.

Six or seven days after the Confession of Peter, Jesus took three disciples and went up to Mount Tabor. As he was praying Jesus was transfigured before his disciples. "The appearance of his face changed...shone like the sun, and his clothes became as white as the light."

Peter was enthused or rather overwhelmed by the overabundant glory of Christ and, not knowing what he was saying, suggested they build three shelters, one for Christ, one for Moses and one for Elijah. He wanted to keep them up there on the mountain. Perhaps he remembered the Cross that would be waiting below and wished to avoid it.

A bright cloud covered them and the disciples were afraid. They were overcome by sacred awe and fell face down to the ground. Out of the cloud they heard the voice of the Father: "This is my Son, whom I love; with him I am well pleased. Listen to him." He is my beloved Son. Follow him even though he is going toward his passion. While the disciples were in this state of awe, the hand of Jesus touched them. He was alone then. The vision of the Transfigured Savior was over. This most holy scene that human eyes could ever witness was described briefly and clearly by "the eyewitnesses of his majesty" when they "were with him on the sacred mountain." (2 Pet. 1.16f).

In the Transfiguration we have a real *theophany* . The face of Jesus shone like the sun. The divine light filled the human nature of

Christ which became the means to reveal his divinity.

We cannot see the divine fully exposed. That is why it is revealed in the cloud, in the darkness. The cloud is a symbol of divine manifestation and divine glory. Such divine revelation only a few are privileged to see and hear in order to become witnesses and to help us believe.

As Luke notes (9.30-31) Moses and Elijah appeared at the Transfiguration as the main representatives of the Old Testament, speaking about the Passion which awaited Jesus in Jerusalem. Thus in the Transfiguration we have a preview-prophecy of the Passion and of the Glory of Christ.

In the marvelous Transfiguration of the Savior the Apostles and Fathers saw the possibility of our own transfiguration. Man is created in the image of God and the image must reflect the glory of the archetype, the original, of God. We see this reflection of glory in its fullness in the human nature of the Lord on Mount Tabor. There the disciples were not transfigured, but they stood capable of seeing the divine light which filled the person of Christ. They saw the glory of Christ "as they were able to see it according to the hymn of the Church. The ultimate purpose of man's life according to the Fathers is to become able to see the divine light, to see the glory of God as clearly as possible, to sense the grace of God filling one's life with peace and spiritual joy. When anyone reaches so close to God then he or she too, can reflect in his or her person the glory of God. Truly the person who lives according to the will of God is transfigured, becomes different; he reflects outwardly the image, the seal of God which he has within. Nowhere else can the divine be revealed as it can be revealed in a person who is united through faith and love to God.

Paul presents us with the example of Moses. Moses remained on Mount Sinai for forty days praying to God. When he descended to the people below "his face was radiant because he had spoken with the Lord" (Ex.34.29f). In the same way, Paul declares that we, too, like spiritual mirrors, receive and reflect the glory of God, become transfigured and progress constantly from glory to glory until we attain to the likeness of Christ (2 Cor. 3.18). "In the same way, let your light so shine before men" (Mt. 5.16).

The ascetic Fathers especially sought to experience this vision of the divine light by constant ascetic effort, prayer and austere meditation. Such an experience is called *theosis* or participation in the divine glory.

Coming down from the mountain Jesus again instructed his disciples not to speak to anyone about the vision they had seen until Christ was crucified and resurrected from the dead (Mt.17.9). Before the Resurrection and Pentecost no one would have understood the Transfiguration in all of its significance.

After this Jesus spoke to his disciples about the forerunner who came as another Elijah to prepare the ground for the coming of the messiah. People did not accept him and killed him through Herod. The same would happen with the messiah (Mt.17.10-13). A mystery! We already know from Plato that the righteous man is persecuted by the society. The righteous man is not of this world; he is of the truth and the world does not want the truth. Yet the righteous must struggle in the world out of love for the salvation of the world.

The Healing of an Epileptic
(Mt.17.14-21; Mk.9.14-29; Lk.9.37-43)

When they descended from the mountain they again met human suffering and unbelief. The language which Jesus used seems hard but love actually prevailed: "O faithless and perverse generation, how long am I to be with you? How long am I to bear with you?" (Mt.17.17). He healed the epileptic boy and asked for more faith, more prayer and more fasting.

Jesus did not seem to want to preach in Galilee any more. His mind was now set on Jerusalem and on the passion. He had to remind his disciples often about this in order to initiate them into this serious matter. the disciples, however, "did not understand what he meant." Even the Pharisees told Jesus to leave Galilee out of fear of Herod (cf.Lk.13.31-33).

CHAPTER NINE

JESUS IN JUDEA

From the journey to Jerusalem Luke has preserved for us certain events and sayings in his section 9.51-18.29. Much of this material has already been told by Matthew and Mark in a different order and in a somewhat different form. The Evangelists Matthew and Mark simply tell us that "when Jesus had finished these sayings, he went away from Galilee and entered the region of Judea beyond the Jordan" (Mt. 19.1) "and large crowds gathered to him; and again, as his custom was, he taught them" (Mk. 10.1) "and he healed them there" (Mt.19.2). Here again, as in Galilee, Jesus had some discussions with the Pharisees and the teachers of the law about divorce, about children, about eternal life. The questions posed by the Jewish leaders appear a bit more theological than those in Galilee. It should be noted, however, that the Pharisees asked the questions in order to test him and not to learn. They really wanted to destroy him.

Marriage and Divorce
Matthew 19.1-12

"Is it lawful to divorce one's wife for any cause?" This was the Pharisees' question. Jesus referred them to Scripture, which contains the actual will of God. According to Scripture the marriage union is the will of God "from the beginning"; its sacred purpose is a life in mutual love and the perpetuation of the human race. By the will of God, marriage is the closest, strongest, and most sacred bond between two persons united into one. If the harmonious coexistence among people is imperative for life, then the marriage union is sacred and a matter of doctrinal principle requires it to remain unbroken. "Therefore what God has joined together, let man not separate." Marriage is sacred and its dissolution is inconceiveable for the believer. If ever we reach the point of divorce, this means that the man, the woman or both did not consider seriously the meaning and the divine purpose of marriage. They did not attempt to maintain the bond sacred. They did not search deeply to find and to understand the will of God behind the institution of marriage and to see the spirit of God in all its depth. Even the thought alone of the divine origin of marriage can help a couple maintain their marriage sacred, respectable and unbroken, in spite of the difficulties which life necessarily presents. The law, as an external force can never grant or guarantee the sacredness of marriage. Many times laws are issued "for our hard-heartedness," since there is no real love and no true sense of our duty. The only way to keep marriage sacred and at the same time enjoyable is to constantly found it upon the will of God with mutual love and respect.

Life Eternal and the Wealth of the World
Matthew 19.16-30; Mark 10.17-31; Luke 18.18-30

"Teacher, what good deed must I do to have eternal life?" A young man who was rich asked this question of Jesus. He wanted to know how to acquire eternal life, to enter the kingdom of God. This is a question which secretly haunts every person, but which rarely is put seriously. We are afraid to see life face to face with its beauty and its questions, with its imperfections and the dissatisfaction which it contains in itself.

Jesus answered the young man: "If you want to enter into life, obey the commandments." Without thinking carefully the young man easily replied: "All these I have kept since I was a boy." We all give the same reply in light conversation about our spiritual life, or even in our confession. We have formulated the notion that we are "good people." We keep the commandments of God, if not in a positive form as love, at least in their negative form: we have not wronged nor killed anybody! And yet the roots of life are much deeper. The young man who was thirsty for life believed he had kept the commandments of God, but in his heart he was not satisfied. This is why he asked: "What do I still lack?" Man is created for perfection and he will always ask "What do I still lack?" What more must I do to be more perfect, more certain that I have eternal life?" This is the question which we need to ponder all the time and this question is the springboard for every progression in our life. Only Christ, "the good teacher," can answer the difficult question of this young man. Only the perfect can speak about the perfect. We can only listen and improve our life constantly, because in this life we cannot attain complete perfection.

"If you would be perfect, go, sell what you possess and give to the poor, and you will have treasure in heaven, and come, follow me" (Mt.19.21). When the young man heard this he became very sad and went away "because he had great wealth." Jesus then drew the conclusion for all of us: "It will be hard for a rich man to enter the kingdom of heaven," and to have eternal life. It is not, however, completely impossible. "With men this is impossible, but with God all things are possible" (Mt.19.21-26). Only when we have God to help us can we be saved even with our wealth, i.e. by using it according to the will of God, like Abraham did.

These words of Jesus appear to be harsh and cause us to ponder: Should we take them literally or relatively? Jesus said these things, and whatever Jesus says we must in the first place take literally, or rather according to the principle meaning of the words. This is why the disciples were astonished and asked, "Who then can be saved?" In this case Christ spoke personally to a young man who wanted to be perfect, and perfect in the Christian life really means this: to abandon everything and to follow freely the only one who is, humanly speaking, perfect, Christ. This is what Peter attempted to say for the disciples: "We have left everything and followed you! What then shall we have?" (Mt.19.27). Man is always looking toward the perfect, toward God. But as long as he is tied down with possessions of the world his heart will certainly be divided between God and such worldly possessions. Thus he cannot really follow Christ, and be his apostle. Unfortunately, the more possessions one has, the more he becomes attached to them. There are, of course, the exceptions. These are the cases where "with God all things are possible." These people will receive in return "one hundred fold in this age and in the future age they shall receive eternal life" (cf.Lk.22.29-30).

Generally, the words of Christ about wealth teach us that our tendency to seek wealth and all worldly glories is an obstacle to a life dedicated to God. Christ told us the same thing with those other words: "you cannot serve two masters." To the extent that one is liberated from the thirst for wealth, he can love God and his neighbor. The criterion of the quality of life is the freedom from earthly possessions and desires on the one hand and the spontaneous love for God and neighbor on the other. The more one loves, the more one lives. Forget yourself as much as possible for the sake of others. Lose your life for others and you will gain it; you will really live here and now and forever near the eternal God of love. Let us all be watchful of the degree of our love, and let us not be complacent with a simple observance of the law and particularly in its merely negative form. For many who consider themselves to be first according to the law in this life may find themselves to be last before the eyes of God. That is how differently from us God sees everything!

The Parable of the Workers in the Vineyard
Matthew 20.1-19

In this parable obviously there is reference to the Jews who believed they were the "first," who had been called and who worked according to the will of God. "Last" are the pagans and the sinners generally. It is these "last" ones that Christ and the Church invite to enter the kingdom of God. The parable wants to show us that the kingdom of God is not a debt owed, wages to be collected, as the Jews believed. The kingdom of God is a gift of God freely given when we love him. We simply must offer our hearts and God gives as much as he wants. He wants and will give life. We see something similar to the attitude of the Jews in the attitude of the elder brother in the parable of the prodigal son (Lk.15.29).

The kingdom of God is a vineyard, and we are the vineyard of God. God wants us all to work as much as we can, according to the gift and the opportunity given to each of us in life. We must all work with faith, love and goodness, not with selfishness and envy toward each other. God who is all good will satisfy all of us. The kingdom of God does not work with contracts and strikes but with love.

The parable of the talents is written with the same spirit (Lk.19. 11-27).

On the Road to Jerusalem
Mark 10.32-34; Matthew 20.17-28

The days of the Passion were coming near. Jesus and his disciples were on their way to Jerusalem.

"We are going up to Jerusalem," he said,"and the Son of Man will be betrayed to the chief priests and teachers of the law. They will condemn him to death and will hand him over to the Gentiles, who will mock him and spit on him, flog him and kill him. Three days later he will rise" (Mk.10.33-34).

Luke adds: "The disciples did not understand any of this (Lk.18. 34). The disciples indeed did not understand what Jesus was telling them. They did not, it appears, want to hear about the cross and were afraid to ask (Mk.9.32). Thus they did not understand well the Passion nor the Resurrection. Their minds went instead immediately to the glory of the kingdom of the messiah. They could picture his enthronement ahead now, to become a reality as soon as they would enter Jerusalem. Human weakness awoke and the sons of Zebedee, either alone or through their mother asked for the first two positions: "Let one of us sit at your right and the other at your left in your glory" (Mk.10.37). "When the ten heard about this, they became indignant with James and John"(Mk.10. 41). "You don't know what you are asking," Jesus said. "Can you drink the cup I drink or be baptized with the baptism I am baptized with?" (Mk.10.38). The "cup" and the "baptism" were symbols for Jesus' impending death. With them he reminded the disciples that the throne and the cross, the kingdom and the sacrifice of love go together. But the cross would come first!

The two disciples, anxious as they were for the positions of honor, answered Jesus' inquiry hastily: "We can." Surely they didn't realize the deep meaning of Christ's words. For when someone really accepts the cross of sacrificial love, then he ceases to think about positions of honor. This is what Christ constantly reminded his disciples: "Whoever wants to become great among you must be your servant, and whoever wants to be first must be a slave of all. For even the Son of Man did not come to be served, but to serve, and to give his life as a ransom for many" (Mk 10.43-45).

How different is the spirit of God from the spirit of men! The work of Christ and of the Church is the service of salvation of the world to the point of self-sacrifice, if necessary. Where we shall sit near God is no problem. The problem is only to be worthy to simply sit near God! The more we offer ourselves to the purpose of Christ and his Church, the more we sense our "little throne" near him. Perhaps this is why John in Revelation sees the many thrones surrounding the one throne (4.4), so that no one can complain. There is room for all near God, and all the places are illumined by the glory of God and of the Lamb.

The Blind Beggar and Zacchaeus
Luke 18.35-19.10

As Jesus and his disciples approached Jericho, a blind man confessed that Jesus is "Son of David", i.e. messiah. "Immediately he received his sight and followed Jesus, praising God" (Lk.18.43).

In Jericho also Jesus was recognized by the tax collector Zacchaeus. Jesus stayed in his house that day and told him:

Today salvation has come to this house, because this man, too, is a son of Abraham. For the Son of Man came to seek and to save what was lost (Lk.19.7-10).

Thus two more men from different social classes in life recognized Christ and found salvation. Still another even more dynamic example is given to us by John in the healing of the man born blind (Jn.9.1-40).

CHAPTER TEN

EVENTS REPORTED BY ST. JOHN

It is difficult to determine where exactly in the life of Christ to place these events. According to the Synoptics, Christ left Galilee for Jerusalem and the cross. Therefore the Synoptics bring us directly to the triumphal entry of Jesus into Jerusalem and then to the Passion. In similar fashion John leads us from Jerusalem directly to the miracle of the feeding of the multitude of the five thousand (6.1,5). Even though John foresaw the cross (6.71), he includes, prior to the triumphal entry into Jerusalem, certain incidents in the life of Christ. Indeed, John pays particular attention to the activity of Jesus in Jerusalem. It is there where the final judgment will take place (Lk.9.58,13.33).

Although he usually pays little attention to the historical continuity of the events, John here has preserved for us certain events which bear witness to the person of Christ, such as the feeding of the five thousand. This, after all, is the purpose of the Gospels: to present the person of Christ so that we may believe in him (20.30-31). In these next sections it is worthwhile to meditate upon what we can learn about Christ from the historical events St. John has selected and placed here.

The Time of Christ
John 7.2-9

According to St. John the feeding of the five thousand took place around the time of the Passover, that is, in the spring. Seven months later, in October, comes the other great feast of the Jews, the Feast of the Tabernacles. The "brothers" of Jesus urged him to go up to Jerusalem to reveal himself officially during the Feast, since he believed himself to be the messiah (7.2-5). Jesus, however, commented that his "time" had not yet come. The "time" of Christ is the hour of the cross. The cross will lead to glory. But this hour of the cross is determined only by the Father and not by men (2.4;7.30).

In Jerusalem the people were waiting for him. Many conversed about his person, and, as always, the opinions of the people were divided. The people wanted to believe and they inquired anxiously: "Where is he?" It was at a great Feast that the messiah was expected to come. But the people were afraid to express their faith because of the Jewish leaders. It is interesting to note here that St. John distinguishes three categories: a) the people in general; b) the Jerusalemites, and c) the leaders (Scribes and Pharisees) which he usually terms "the Jews."

"If a Man is Thirsty, Let Him Come to Me and Drink" John 7.37-39

In response to this thirst for a messiah-savior, Jesus went up to Jerusalem and while there he exclaimed:

"If a man is thirsty, let him come to me and drink. Whoever believes in me, as the Scripture has said, streams of living water will flow from within him" (7.37-38).

St. John explains that by these words Jesus meant the Holy Spirit who would be sent by Christ to the Church after the cross and the resurrection to refresh and to save the souls of the believers (7.37-39).

The people believed; the leaders not only disbelieved, but planned to seize Jesus by sending out the temple guards When the temple guards returned without Jesus, the leaders asked them anxiously: "Why didn't you bring him in?" And the guards retorted: "No one ever spoke the way this man does" (7.45-48). At this point Nicodemos apparently tried to help but to no avail (7.50-52). The hatred of disbelief was obvious; they wanted to condemn him without a hearing!

At this critical point, St. John presents the story of the adulteress to show on one hand the total poverty of the justice of the law, and, on the other, the height of the law of divine love which seeks not to condemn but to save man (Jn.3.17,7.53-58.11).

At this point St. John has included a series of controversies with the Jewish leaders (8.12-10.39). Christ speaks more clearly about himself and he is more critical and more offensive than he was earlier in Galilee. The most important points of the dialogue are the following:

"I Am the Light of the World"
John 8.12

Jesus appeared again, after the events in Jn.7.37 and said:

I am the light of the world. Whoever follows me will never walk in darkness, but will have the light of life (Jn.8.12,cf.1.4-9).

Jesus as the messiah is the guiding light which man needs to follow in order not to be lost in the darkness of life. Indeed he is even to-day and forever "the true light which gives light to every man" (1.9). Without the light of Christ, no healthy civilization can exist in the world. Unfortunately, however, the world as a whole did not accept the light. People preferred the darkness to the light. This was the complaint of St. John in 1.10-11, 3.19, 12.43. The leaders doubted this self-testimony of Jesus and did not accept the light.

Then Jesus testifies that he comes from God and that the Father who sent him also testifies on his behalf (8.18). Jesus accuses them, saying that they do not "know the Father" and for this reason they do not know the Son either (8.19). He invites them to believe. It is the final moment before the cross and they must not lose this opportunity.

"I am with you for only a short time, and then I go to the one who sent me" (Jn.7.33). "Where I go, you cannot come...if you do not believe that I am he (the messiah), you will indeed die in your sins" (Jn.8.21,24).

The Jewish leaders misunderstood Jesus on both occasions, when he said "I am with you for only a short time, and where I go, you cannot come." Unknowingly, they predicted the significance of his sacrificial death on the cross. The death on the cross was a self sacrifice. Christ would "kill himself" for the people, for the Greeks and the entire world (7.35,8.22). When John was writing, the Gospel of Christ had indeed reached the Greeks.

With these words some believed. Christ advised them to remain faithful to his words, to learn the truth and the truth would make them free from the slavery of sin and every human weakness. This freedom is given only by the Son who is always at home together with the Father. Human self esteem reacted to Jesus' comments about slavery: "We are Abraham's descendants and have never been slaves of anyone" (8.33). Then Jesus answered them:

You are not the Children of Abraham because you do not think and act as he did. Neither are you of God because you do not know my words which are the words of God. You are from below, from the world. You are the children of the devil (8.37-47).

"Before Abraham Was Born, I Am
John 8.58

The Jews indicted Jesus, calling him a heretical Samaritan possessed by a demon. Jesus called them to repentance and faith for their salvation:

I tell you the truth, if a man keeps my word, he will never see death...Your father Abraham rejoiced at the thought of seeing my day... I tell you the truth, before Abraham was born, I am (8.58. cf. Heb.11.13-19; Gen.21.3,17.19).

Jesus revealed that he was eternal; he existed before Abraham and before the world. When the world began to be created, Christ already was, he existed eternally together with the Father (Jn.1. 1-2).

The result of this heated exchange? "They picked up stones to stone him" (8.59). Jesus tried to tell them that he was the one their father Abraham expected and they tried to stone him! Jesus slipped away and hid from them. Thus Jesus remains hidden to those who do not believe.

The following story of the blind man is an illustrated example of the blindness of these leaders.

Jesus Heals a Man Born Blind
John 9.1-38

When Jesus and his disciples met on the road a man blind from birth, the disciples asked why he had been born blind. Jesus replied that this blindness was an opportunity "that the work of God might be made manifest in his life" (9.3). WIth this miracle of healing one more soul was saved. The blind man became another witness to the divine truth which the religious leaders of Israel could not see. And now Jesus, as if tired himself, allowed the blind man to carry out the struggle of defense on his own behalf. The man who had had no sight told the wise that Christ was the spiritual light. His defense was simple, clear and impressive. He spoke from experience, from his healing. He knew too well that Jesus could not be a deceiver. For Jesus to have done such a unique miracle and to have opened his eyes, had to have been a "godly man who does the will of God; he must be a prophet." The Pharisees retorted that they did not "know" Jesus as a good man. But the blind man again defended Jesus:

Now that is remarkable! You don't know where he comes from, yet he opened my eyes...If this man were not from God, he could do nothing" (9.18,25,29-33).

I Am the Judgment
John 9.39-41

The leaders insulted the blind man and threw him out, cut him off from the synagogue, the only negative thing they could do. Jesus later found the blind man again and revealed to him that he is the messiah. The man believed and worshiped Christ. And with this the spiritual completion of the healing took place. Now Jesus, seeing the change in the blind man on the one hand and the stubborn disbelief in the leaders on the other, said:

For judgment I have come into this world, so that the blind will see and those who see will become blind (Jn.9.39).

In this story we indeed learn that it is many times better to be "blind," to know that we do not know many things. Socrates once said: "I know one thing, that I don't know anything." In such a

situation our heart remains open to receive the good and it can receive the rays of divine truth which always come from above, by
revelation. When we stubbornly insist that we know everything,
we cannot approach the light and may even block others from approaching it, thus impeding the very work of Christ and the
Church. We project ourselves instead of Christ and his Church.

Faith essentially is not so much a matter of knowledge as it is
a matter of ethics, a matter of obedience, or disobedience to the
will of God. Divine truth indeed shone as light in the person of
Christ (2 Cor.4.3-6). Those who do not accept Christ as light seek
to project themselves and not the truth. This is their judgment and
their sin (Jn.15.22-25; 3.17-21,36; 5.24).

I Am the Good Shepherd
John 10

In chapters seven and eight we saw how the leaders placed ob-
stacles in the way of the people's believing in Christ and having
the light of life. In chapter nine where the blind man spoke about
Jesus, the leaders put him out of the synagogue. In chapter 10
now Christ criticizes the leaders as exploiters of the flock. The
image of the flock is very popular among the Jewish people (Is.40.
11; Mt.18.12; Jn.21.15). The Prophet Ezekiel (34.1-31) clearly
prophecied that God was concerned for his flock, for his people
and would one day sent the good shepherd to save his sheep. With
this familiar image for the Jews, Christ now judged the leaders as
shepherds of the people of God, and declared that he is the good
shepherd whom God has sent to save his sheep. The image is indeed a vivid one as it comes out of real life. The sheep need the
corral where they are sheltered from the cold, from the beasts and
from thieves. There is the real shepherd and there is the hireling
shepherd. There are also the thieves and the beasts of prey.

In this image-parable, Christ is the door of the sheep. Anyone
who wants to be a shepherd of the people of God must pass by
Christ; he must approach the sheep in and through Christ. All
things must begin from Christ and must move toward Christ so
that the sheep, the people of God, may have life in abundance.

"All who came before me" (all who attempted to approach the people without Christ) "were thieves and robbers" who sought "only to steal and kill and destroy." The sheep did not recognize them and did not follow (10.7-10).

The hireling shepherds, too, may approach the sheep through Christ and the sheep may recognize them and follow them. The trouble with hireling shepherds is that sometimes they do not love the sheep as their own; they do not see them as the beloved sheep of God for which Christ died. That is why when they see danger, when they see the "wolves" coming, they abandon the sheep and run away, and "the wolf attacks the flock and scatters it" (10. 13).

The entire parable-image emphasizes the great responsibility of those who wish to be leaders of the people and particularly of religious leaders. The work of a leader is actually sacred, but when it is not carried out according to God it is outright robbery. The leaders bear all the responsibility for the corruption of the people.

"I am the good shepherd" (10.14-18). Finally, Jesus presented the picture of the good shepherd. With the familiar image of Ezekiel (34.23-24), Jesus declared that he is the good shepherd, the expected messiah, descendent of David, sent by God to save the flock—ready to give even his life for the life of the sheep. With these comments, Christ alluded to his approaching cross. And with these words there was again a division among the Jews (10.19-21).

Two months later in December at the Feast of Hanukkah, the Dedication of the Temple, the Jews challenged Jesus to tell them openly if he was the messiah. "How long will you keep us in suspense? If you are the Christ, tell us plainly" (Jn.10.24). Jesus knew that they did not really have the will to believe. He knew that they were not from among his sheep. For this reason he made no effort to help them believe. He directly cut them off: "You do not believe because you are not my sheep" (10.26). The Father has not given you to me.

The Theology of Chapter 10

If we observe a bit more analytically the words of John in chapter ten, we shall see that in every expression he has something deeper to tell us of the person and the work of Christ. However, John presupposes much familiar kerygmatic material from the life of the Church and expresses his thoughts quite freely, therefore, it is sometimes difficult to follow him. The same thing happens with the doctrines of the Church. Those who have no knowledge of the whole life of the Church are surprised by the way of thinking of the Church and find it difficult to understand and to accept as truth this doctrine in its brief, but clear, formulation. For those, however, who live the life of the Church and share in her struggles and her problems, the doctrines are so natural, so clear and logical.

In chapter ten Christ appears as the good shepherd who gives his life for the salvation of his sheep. But this has its roots in the deeper relationship which exists between Christ and the sheep, and, on an even deeper level, between Christ and the Father, and between the Father and the sheep—the people.

Christ is the good shepherd and he gives his life for the sheep because he knows them as his own.

> I am the good shepherd; I know my sheep and my sheep know me—just as the Father knows me and I know the Father—and I lay down my life for the sheep (10.14-15).

In the language of faith this mutual knowledge is not a rational, theoretical kind of knowledge, but contains in itself an ontological element. It is existential knowledge; it is an experience of relationship and of life. The Son knows the sheep because they are his. He created them (Jn.1.3,10). The believers know Christ as the source of their life and they live because of their mystical "knowledge-union" with Christ (Jn.6.56-57,15.1f). Christ too, lives for the sheep—the believers. This is why he became man and came to us. From the nativity to the crucifixion, he "lays down his life for the sheep." With the cross and resurrection, the glory of the son as savior was to be fulfilled. It was then that he would draw all mankind to himself, he would gather together all the other sheep so that there would be one flock, the people and the kingdom of God, with one shepherd, Christ, to the glory of God the Father (Jn.12.32,cf.Phil.2.6-11).

This relationship between the shepherd and the flock has its root in the deeper relationship of the Father and the Son. The Son gives life to the sheep because of his relationship with the Father.

The Father knows the Son and the Son knows the Father. The Son lives eternally with the mutual knowledge he has with the Father. The life of the Holy Trinity is an eternal relationship of mutual knowledge and love (6.56-57,10.3,15,38). Thus our union with the Incarnate Son of God unites us with that uncreated Divinity (17.23), the only source of life. Our life is a life that has its source in the mystery of the Holy Trinity. "For in him we live and move and have our being." (Acts 17.28). The Son became man in order to save man, to help him root his life in God. The sacrifice of Christ on the cross is an expression—the will—of the infinite love of the Triune God for the salvation of the world. In the salvation in Christ we have the revelation of God the Father who works eternally to save the world through the Son. This is the subject of the Gospel.

I and the Father Are One
John 10.17-18, 27-30

The Son came to the world and gave his life for the life of the sheep because this was the will and commandment of the Father. But the will of the Father is also the Son's will. This is what Jesus meant when he spoke about his life:

No one takes it from me, but I lay it down of my own accord. I have authority to lay it down and authority to take it up (10.18).

The Son's sheep are also the Father's. The Father is together with the Son and this is a guarantee that the work of salvation will succeed.

My sheep listen to my voice; I know them, and they follow me. I give them eternal life, and they shall never perish; no one can snatch them out of my hand. My Father, who has given them to me, is greater than all; no one can snatch them out of my Father's hand. I and the Father are one (10.27-30).

The expression "I and the Father are one," does not mean identity merely in will and energy but also in essence. The essential identity of the Triune God is where the Gospel of John begins and where it ends with the expression of Thomas: "my Lord and my God" (1.1,20.28-29). For the Jews, though this was a blasphemous expression and they tried to stone Jesus (10.31-33). Christ, however, slipped away from them, and in John this is really the last time that Jesus speaks to the Jews.

After the personal conflict with the Jews, Jesus went into the desert where John was first baptizing: Jesus returned to where he had started his work. Many followers of John confessed that Jesus was indeed greater than John. "And in that place many believed in Jesus" (Jn.10.42). The last impressions confirmed the first (cf.1 29,3.29,10.40-42). From this place Jesus would again return to Jerusalem when the hour of the cross sounded.

Christ—The Resurrection and the Life
John 11

There in the desert Jesus was informed that his friend Lazarus was ill. Jesus further delayed his departure and Lazarus died. On the fourth day Jesus arrived in Bethany. The disciples, knowing the hatred of the Jews, tried to prevent him from going to Jerusalem. Finally, of course, they actually followed him with some premonitions (11.16). Martha and Mary, the sisters of Lazarus met Jesus outside the town. Jesus was deeply moved by their great grief and decidedly headed for the grave (11.20-38). He would do the miracle-sign which would testify that the resurrection and the eternal life of people depends upon faith in Christ (11.21-22).

"Your brother will rise again." Yes, but when? At the last day? At the general resurrection which all pious Jews await? Then Jesus answered:

I am the resurrection and the life. He who believes in me will live, even though he dies; and whoever lives and believes in me will never die (11.25-26).

Christ is life. This was precisely what he wanted the miracle to testify. Where Christ is present we have the presence of resurrection and life. In his presence death loses its meaning for the believer. Christ is life, and whoever is united with life does not fear the possibility of losing it. Life is God's gift in response to our faith in Christ. This life is enjoyed by the believer now through his relationship with Christ, and he will live it more perfectly and completely after the general resurrection when "we will be with the

Lord forever" (1 Thess. 4.17). "Do you believe this?" Jesus asked
Martha, and Martha confessed her faith in Christ as the Jews of
that time expected him."Yes, Lord, I believe that you are the
Christ, the Son of God who is coming into the world" as Lord Savior (11.27).

The incident before the tomb of Lazarus is depicted dramatical-
ly in 11.39-44. Martha was fearful. Jesus challenged her to greater
faith, greater than that which we can usually have. He requires
faith that feels the presence of God, and sees his glory. Jesus
raised his eyes in prayer, which was another prayerful appeal to
the people to believe (11.41-42).
"Lazarus, come out!" The unheard of took place! And John
gives us the details: "The dead man came out..."Take off the
grave clothes and let him go!"

After the miracle, Jesus did not speak to the people. The miracle, however, testifies that Jesus is the messiah coming into the
world as victor over death and provider of true life. The resurrection of Lazarus is a living image-parable of the general resurrection
of the dead as described in John 5.28-29. This is the purpose of
the miracle. Every other human thought upon this event pales by
comparison.

What was the result? Many believed. Others ran to the Pharisees.
The leaders decided to kill Jesus. It was necessary for one man to
die for all the people. And John sees this decision as an involun-
tary prophecy—that Christ would actually die for the people, not
as the Jewish leaders had imagined it, but for the whole world as
the eternal love of God had fore-ordained (3.16,11.45-53).

Again Jesus retreated toward the desert to wait for his hour to
come. And the hour came with the great Feast of Passover, when
"many went up from the country to Jerusalem." In two lines John
describes the hearts of the crowd. Some sought to find him and to
accept him as the messiah; others to seize him and kill him (11,55-
57)! All these details prepare us to follow the events of the great
and holy week of the passion.

The Supper in Bethany
John 12.1-8; Matthew 26.6-13; Mark 14.3-9

John speaks of the supper in Bethany before the triumphal en-

try of Jesus into Jerusalem. Matthew and Mark place the same
story four days later. It is possible that this could be a second supper. The Evangelists are not interested in absolute historical accuracy. They are primarily interested in the teaching of faith, in the
testimony for the person of Christ and not so much in the testimony of other persons. We shall follow John because his narrative
is somewhat more historical than the others. John connected the
triumphal entry with the miracle of Lazarus which played a decisive
role both for many to believe in Christ and for the Pharisees'
leaders to decide to kill Jesus. Thus John presents a more festive,
lively atmosphere around Jesus' reception in Jerusalem than do
the Synoptics.

Lazarus, whom Jesus raised from the dead, was one of those who
sat at that supper. Martha, as we know, was the one who served.
But Mary also served with her particular devotion to Christ (Lk.
10.38-42). Piety and love made Mary pour the most precious perfume on the feet of Christ. The whole house was filled with the
fragrance of the perfume. Judas Iscariot was troubled by this out-
pouring of love. He would have preferred to sell the perfume and
with the money to help many poor people. Many philanthropists
of today would have thought the same way. John, however, notes
that Judas' motive was not love for the poor but his greed; at least
this is how he appeared later at the betrayal. The Synoptics also
related this reference with the betrayal of Judas (Mt.26.14-16).
Jesus stood up for the woman.

'Leave her alone,' Jesus replied. 'It was meant that she should
save this perfume for the day of my burial. You will always
have the poor among you, but you will not always have me' (Jn.
12.7-8).

Do not disturb the woman. Do not think about the waste of the
perfume. The poor will always be with you and if you really love
them you will find some way to help them. Here Jesus thinks of
his imminent death and adds the remark that he will not be much
longer with them. Mary's love for Jesus caused her to use the perfume which was meant for the day of his burial. Her deed was considered an anticipatory anointing, a foreshadowing of the coming
death. We know historically that the women did not in fact have
the opportunity to anoint the body of Jesus in the tomb; he was
already resurrected when they arrived at the empty tomb. Thus he

who gave life to the dead Lazarus was himself now being anointed as dead. But also it was as an anointed king that Jesus proceeded to Jerusalem.

The question of Judas about the poor is a great concern of many today, and it is difficult for the Church to explain satisfactorily the luxury which often characterizes its life. The beautiful scene and particularly the words of Christ will always remind us that the sincere expression of our love for God, even with apparent luxury, should not be condemned. On the contrary, such a sincere expression of love and respect can easily lead us toward love and help for our neighbor. Love toward God and neighbor increase together, and alone neither of them can exist. If we could all love Christ then there would be fewer poor, *and the Judases would be non-existent.*

It is true that God does not require luxuries for worship. Rather these are sought by the soul as a means to express its love for God. We need to decorate our homes to add beauty and joy to our life. In the same manner we need to decorate the house of the Lord which belongs to all of us and everything in it must be as immaculate and perfect as possible. We see this in all the religious monuments throughout the world. The problem, however, is when we lose ourselves in the beauty and forget the life of faith. Let us all be careful of this!

The Triumphal Entry Into Jerusalem
John 12.9-19; Matthew 21.1-9; Mark 11.1-10; Luke 19.28-38

Here John meets with the synoptics. He gives us a lively description of the scene. Many people came to Bethany to see Jesus and Lazarus who had been raised from the dead. These were the people who would accompany Jesus to the great Feast of Passover in Jerusalem. On the other hand there was also the dark scene of the high-priests who considered killing Lazarus, too, because his presence moved many people to believe in Christ. Other people in Jerusalem itself heard of Jesus' coming and went out to meet him outside the city walls.

When the procession neared the Mount of Olives, Christ sent two disciples to bring a donkey. The owner was apparently a per-

son known from previous visits and he gave the donkey. Jesus sat
on the donkey and proceeded to Jerusalem. Only after the Resurrection did the disciples understand that this had happened because this was how the Prophet Zacharias had prophecied the
coming of the Messiah-King:

> Say to the Daughter of Zion, 'See, your king comes to you, gen-
> tle and riding on a donkey.'

> A very large crowd spread their cloaks on the road, while others
> cut branches from the trees and spread them on the road. The
> crowds that went ahead and those that followed shouted, "Ho-
> sanna to the Son of David! Blessed is he who comes in the name
> of the Lord! Hosanna in the highest" (Mt.21.4-9; Ps.118.25)!

When the procession reached Jerusalem "the whole city was
stirred and asked 'who is this?'"(Mt.21.10). Jesus had visited Jerusalem before, but he had never been received like this. The people
received Jesus as the "Son of David," the King of Israel, the one
sent by God as Savior and Messiah (Mk.11.10).

The high priests and the Pharisees wanted Jesus to stop the disciples, the people, and the children from receiving him as the Messiah. And Jesus replied: "If they keep quiet, the stones will cry
out" (Lk.19.40). Has it not been said by the prophet, 'From the
lips of children and infants you have ordained praise'?" (Mt.21.16;
Ps.8.2).

Jesus visited the Temple but because it was late he and his disciples left and went out to Bethany to spend the night.

CHAPTER ELEVEN

THE LAST WEEK

The next day Jesus again came to Jerusalem. On the way he noticed a single fig tree, and being hungry he approached it, hoping to find some figs to eat. He found nothing on the tree except leaves. He then cursed the tree saying, "May you never bear fruit again!" On the next day the fig tree was completely withered. This incident has been preserved as a symbolic act. Neither was the season right for figs, nor the curse appropriate to the love of Christ. It was rather a symbolic prophecy against the Jews. The piety of the Jews had "leaves only," many external practices but no fruit, no true godly piety. This was demonstrated right afterward with the cleansing of the Temple. The destruction of the fig tree symbolizes the judgment which was to come upon Israel. Shortly after, Jesus related this event to the power of true prayer (Mk.11.20-25).

The Cleansing of the Temple
Matthew 21.12-13; Mark 11.14-19

Christ proceeded to the Temple and saw its courtyard transformed into a place of business. With amazing authority he drove out everyone and everything, saying: "This house of God is a place of prayer, but you have made it into a place of business." The abrupt manner by which this event is introduced here by the Evangelists indicates that it had happened before. The merchants had previously experienced his power. In John 2.13-22 we have a more colorful description of a similar scene.

This phenomenon of business in the house of God is to be
found today in many religious festivals and it weakens to a great
extent the religious feelings of many of our people. The mainte-
nance of the Church does require money. But care should be
taken in *how* we acquire this money and that we do so without
weakening the faith of our people. Contributions should be truly
a spontaneous thanksgiving for the goods we receive from God.

Various Conversations With the Jewish Leaders
Matthew 21.14-46

With a few words the Evangelists describe for us the work of
Christ during those days:

> Each day Jesus was teaching at the temple, and each evening he
> went out to spend the night on the hill called the Mount of
> Olives, and all the people came early in the morning to hear him
> at the temple (Lk.21.37).

The people marveled at his teaching and were literally hanging
from his every word.

"By What Authority Are You Doing These Things?"
Matthew 21.23-27

The high priests and the teachers of the Law, however, sought
how to kill him (Mk.11.18; Lk.19.47-48,21.37-38). The leaders
were no longer willing to listen to him; they simply wanted to
"trap" him with some word and to condemn him. For this reason
they first asked him: "By what authority are you doing these
things?...and who gave you this authority" to teach and to expel
the people from the Temple? The right answer would have been:
My authority comes from above, from my Father; I act as the Messiah, the Son sent by God. Something like this he had told them
in John seven through ten. But the leaders would never believe
this. Therefore Jesus responded now with another question. He
challenged them to express their opinion about the mission of
John the Baptist. They could not answer because they had not
taken seriously the message of John or of Jesus. Then Christ told

them "Neither will I tell you by what authority I am doing these things" (Mt.21.23-27). With a parable Jesus exposed the leaders as unrepentent hypocrites. They prided themselves on their piety as the beloved children of God, while in reality they did not live according to the will of God. "I tell you the truth, the tax collectors and the prostitutes are entering the kingdom of God ahead of you" (Mt.21.31). With the parable of the evil farmers (Mt.21.33-46), Jesus indicted the leaders for being poor stewards of the gifts of God. They had killed the Prophets and were now ready to kill even the Son of God, the Messiah. With the judgment: "He will bring those wretches to a wretched end," the leaders of Judaism signed their own indictment.

The vineyard is a popular image in the Bible. The vineyard of God is Israel (Is.5.1-7; Ps.80.8f). God chose Israel as his beloved people and waited for the fruits of faith and piety. Unfortunately, neither the people nor the leaders produced fruit. Thus came the threat of destruction. The vineyard would be given to another nation, or rather in Christ we would have the new vineyard, the Church, the true Israel, the kingdom of God.

Here another parable is added from Psalm 118.22-23. The builders of theocratic Israel rejected one stone which they considered useless. In the end, however, and according to the will of God, this stone became the cornerstone on which the whole edifice rested. This stone is Christ, whom the Jewish leaders rejected, but who became the cornerstone of the Church that was to unite the whole world into one (1Pet.2.6-8; 1Cor.3.11; Eph.2.20). The leaders with their opposition would be crushed and scattered as dust. The words are harsh; the story was familiar to the Jews and the leaders realized that he was speaking about them. No wonder they wanted to seize him quickly. Yet, they feared the people who considered Jesus to be a great Prophet.

The Parable of the Royal Wedding
Matthew 22.1-14

Another popular image for the kingdom of God and the messiah is the wedding and the wedding banquet. In the Old Testament the relationship of God toward his people is presented as a marriage relationship. In the New Testament the close bond between the believers and Christ is symbolized by the image of marriage (Song of Songs 8; Eph.5.25; Rev.19.9). At this critical time just before the cross, Christ told the parable of the wedding of the king's son to challenge them to repent, to wear the "wedding garments" of virtues and to enter worthily into the wedding chamber. If they would not repent, judgment awaited them. The Jewish leaders not only did not believe but they also mistreated and even killed the kings's servants. This is why the frightful judgment came without delay. "The king was enraged. He sent his army and destroyed those murderers and burned their city" (Mt.22.7). The parable ends with the observation: "For many are invited, but few are chosen." God invites all of us to his kingdom, but he wants us to live a life worthy of our calling as royal children of God. St. John Chrysostom once said that "the wedding garment is our way of life; and while to be invited and to be cleansed is the work of God's grace, to remain clean is the work of the guests."

Caesar's Coin
Luke 20.20-26; Matthew 22.15-22

The leaders not only did not repent but they constantly attempted to "trap" him in some word in order to hand him over to the authorities. They sent spies and perhaps some people loyal to the king to ask Jesus what opinion he had about paying taxes to Rome. "Is it right for us to pay taxes to Caesar or not?" (Lk.20. 22). The zealous Jews considered it a great burden for the people of God to be paying taxes to Rome. If Jesus answered that it was good to pay these taxes, he would not be a faithful Jew. If again he answered no, they would surely condemn him for being against Caesar. Jesus "saw through their duplicity" and gave them the answer which remains to this day a famous proverb: "give to Caesar what is Caesar's, and to God what is God's" (Lk.20.25;cf. Mt.17.24-27). "When they heard this they were amazed. So they left him and went away" (Mt.22.22). They were amazed at Jesus but they did not believe.

Money is something external and it can and should be given as a tax for the needs of the state. To God we owe only faith and love "with all of our hearts." Consequently, for a faithful person, the paying of taxes does not become an obstacle to the faithfulness. Later on, though, in early Church history when the Caesars demanded the faithful to confess that "Caesar is Lord," the Christians said: "No, Jesus Christ is Lord."

Faith in the Resurrection
Matthew 22.23-33

After the conservative Pharisees come some liberal Sadducees who did not believe in the resurrection of the dead as did the Pharisees. Their purpose was to prove the foolishness of the belief in the resurrection. To do this they presented a hypothetical situation to Jesus. A woman was married to seven men consecutively. If we believe that there is resurrection and life after death, the problem will arise as to which of the seven husbands will have the woman. Jesus answered harshly but didactically. "You are in error because you do not know the Scriptures or the power of God" (Mt.22.29) This is what happens to all of us when we seek to think things out and to draw conclusions about spiritual truths or realities with only the laws of this present life as guides and without the Faith of the Church. When the Scriptures speak about the resurrection they do not refer to reason but to the unlimited power and will of God which no one can fathom. St. Paul tells us that spiritual truths must be compared and understood only with spritual criteria (1 Cor.2.9-16). This is why Christ continued:

At the resurrection people will neither marry nor be given in marriage; they will be like the angels in heaven (Mt.22.3).

Life after the resurrection will be different, completely new. Our relations will not be as here on earth: relations of marriage, births and death. Then we shall all live as the angels in heaven with love and continual praise of God. This of course does not exclude our knowing and recognizing each other (cf.Lk.16,23).

In order to confirm faith in the resurrection, Christ referred to only one of the Scriptures, very well known to the Saducees also, where God speaks to Moses: "I am the God of (your father) Abraham, the God of Isaac, and the God of Jacob." The God who speaks to Moses *is* also the God of Abraham.The living God is not

God of the dead but of the living. Thus it must be concluded that the soul of Abraham lives and awaits the resurrection.

The First and the Greatest Commandment
Matthew 22.34-40; Mark 12.28-31

After the Sadducees, the Pharisees came again. An expert teacher of the law of Moses asked Jesus which is the greatest commandment in the law. And Jesus replied:

> Love the Lord your God with all your heart and with all your soul and with all your mind. This is the first and greatest commandment. And the second is like it: Love your neighbor as yourself (Mt.22.37-39).

Jesus did not stop at the first commandment but added the second one also. If one interprets well the first one, he also has the second one. If one truly loves God, he must also love his neighbor, his fellow man and woman, the children of God.

> "We love because he first loved us. If anyone says, 'I love God,' yet hates his brother, he is a liar. For anyone who does not love his brother, whom he has seen, cannot love God, whom he has not seen. And he has given us this command: Whoever loves God must also love his brother" (1 Jn.4.19-21).

When love is real it has no bounds; it embraces God and everything; it becomes absolute love, life in God who is love. On this double commandment of love the whole Law and the Prophets are founded. In the spiritual life of believers everything must begin with love and everything must end with love. The teacher of the law who asked the question appeared to have agreed, and Jesus told him that he was not far from the kingdom of God (Lk.20.40).

Luke notes that at this point "no one dared to ask him any more questions." But Jesus asked a question of them and challenged the leaders to think more deeply about the messiah and his messianic kingdom and to take a proper position in regard to him.

The Son of David and Christ
Matthew 22.41-46

The Jews expected the messiah to be a descendent of King David who would restore the Kingdom of Judah in all of its political, moral and religious grandeur. But Christ invited them to think more deeply about the actual relationship between David and the messiah who would bring about this radical change in the nation and in the world. To do this he presented a particular messianic passage:

> How is it then that David, speaking by the Spirit, calls him "Lord"? For he says, "the Lord said to my Lord: Sit at my right hand until I put your enemies under your feet." (Mt.22. 43-44; Ps.110.1).

The Jews considered this psalm to be messianic; they accepted the fact that David spoke "by the spirit" about the messiah and called him "my Lord." The relationship between David·and messiah, then is that the messiah according to the flesh was a descendent of David, but according to the spirit he is the Lord, the Son of God (cf.Rom.1.3-4,9.5).

It appears that the Pharisees could not answer. No one really can answer such great and essential questions of faith if he or she does not live the whole mystery of salvation in Christ as the Church has lived it through the ages.

The Attack on Hypocrisy
Matthew 23.1-36

In this section Matthew presents Christ delivering the fearful "woes" against the hypocrites. Did Jesus say them all at the same time or did he say them on different occasions and Matthew groups this material together as he often does? In any case their essential nature does not change. It is remarkable that Christ, who taught us not to judge, but to forgive and to love all people, delivered these "woes" against hypocrisy and evil when the time and occasion warranted it. This was always done with the purpose and the hope of repentance, of correction, and of salvation. Jesus did not come to judge but to save the world. Even here his voice should be heard as a voice of paternal love, like the one we hear addressed to the elder son in the parable of the prodigal son.

The section, of course, was addressed primarily toward the Jew-

ish leaders who were more responsible for the destiny of the people. But the message should be of interest to all of us. By studying
these passages we can all examine the quality of our faith and our
religious life to see if indeed there is real fear of God and if there is
righteousness and love, or if perhaps ours is merely a religion of
words, of the lips, and of external ostentation. Many of us judge
others and yet in one way or another do the same things: we are
negligent, indifferent, hypocritical and even downright mean
sometimes.

Hypocrisy is a terrible thing in all aspects of life, but it is even
more an abomination when it is found in our religious life. We attempt to deceive God, but God cannot be deceived. "God cannot
be mocked" (Gal.6.7). This is why Christ appears unusually harsh
when he attacks hypocrisy:

The Widow's Two Coins
Mark 12.42; Luke 21.2

After the thunder and lightening of the "woes" against hypocrisy comes the didactic image of the simple pious woman. She was a
poor widow. But her piety made her offer something for the needs
of the Temple. She only had two coins in her possession and she
gave them both. She caught the attention of Jesus who chose to
immortalize her. In the eyes of God the two coins of the widow
have much greater value than the expensive coins offered by the
many. The reason for this is simply that these two coins represent
the spirit of sacrifice; the widow gave everything she had! Without
the spirit of sacrifice everything becomes hypocritical.

The Last Things
Matthew 24.1-25, 46

In chapter twenty-four Matthew has gathered various teachings
which refer to the future. The present had already been judged.
The Jews had not accepted Jesus as the messiah and his crucifixion
was approaching. Jesus was surrounded by his disciples who were
to later continue his work, and they were, at the moment, full of
questions. So Christ spoke about what was to take place in the fu-

ture. He spoke about the future fortune of Jerusalem, about the propagation of the Good News of salvation, about the time when these things would take place, and particularly about his Parousia.

The Destruction of Jerusalem
Matthew 24.1-3; Mark 13.1-4

The disciples looked upon Jerusalem and marveled at its magnificent structures, especially the Temple. This prompted Christ to predict the destruction of Jerusalem. He saw clearly that this destruction would be its final indictment. That is the direction in which the religious as well as the political life of its leaders was going. Jerusalem was the sacred center of Judaism, and many times Christ spoke about it with sadness and love (Lk.13.33-35;19.35-44). Jerusalem was the Holy City of Israel, and yet quite often it persecuted the prophets of God who tried to lead the people to true piety and life, as is appropriate for the chosen people of God. Now they were ready to kill the messiah himself. And Jesus mourned over Jerusalem:

O Jerusalem, Jerusalem, you who kill the prophets and stone those sent to you, how often I have longed to gather your children together, as a hen gathers her chicks under her wings, but you were not willing. Look, your house is left to you desolate. For I tell you, you will not see me again until you say, "Blessed is he who comes in the name of the Lord" (Mt. 23.37-39).

They would not see him; he would not trouble them any more until that time after the Resurrection when they would receive him as the messiah, as the Son of Man, just as the people and the children had received him before. The question remains: Will they repent? Will they believe? Or will they again persecute his Church?

In chapter 24.15-22 the destruction of Jerusalem is described. The grief will be great, "unequaled from the beginning of the world until now--and never to be equaled again" (24.21). In 170 B.C. Jerusalem had been seiged, but the destruction then was not as great as it was in 70 A.D. It is said of this second destruction that about 97,000 were taken captives to Rome.

The End of the World
Matthew 24.1-44; Mark 13.1-37; Luke 21.5-36

The destruction of Jerusalem for the people of that time meant the beginning of the end. After the destruction of Jerusalem the end of the world would come quickly.

The Jewish people expected it; it would be the "Day of the "Lord", "That Day" when God would personally enter the history of the world and a new period would begin for the world: "the new age," "the future age," the messianic kingdom, the kingdom of God on earth.

The disciples of Jesus had similar hopes. And they asked: "When will this happen, and what will be the sign of your coming and of the end of the age?" (Mt.13.2). In response Christ first warned the disciples to be vigilant, not to be misled by the false prophets who would be claiming an imminent coming of the messiah (24.4-5). Before the coming Parousia, he told them, there will be wars, earth-quakes, and other natural catastrophes. *All these will not mark the end*. They will only be the beginning of the suffering (24.4-8).

Another event which will preceed the Parousia is the preaching of the Gospel throughout the whole world. Together with the preaching of the Gospel, however, there will also be persecutions. "If they have persecuted me, they will persecute you also." At the time he said this Christ was experiencing the most difficult persecution. The world will continue to persecute the Gospel because as the true light it censures the wavering life of the people (Mt.24.9-14).

The False Prophets and the Parousia
Matthew 24.23-28; Luke 17.22-35

"Then" — at the time of agony and pain, of social and political upheaval — false prophets and false messiahs will appear to promise salvation or the coming of the messiah. Do not believe them! No one knows the day and the hour of the Parousia of the messiah, the "Son of Man," and it is not even necessary for anyone to tell us about the Parousia, for it will come suddenly just when no one

is expecting it, and, as instantaneous lightening, it will shine from
one end of the world to the other. Do not believe therefore those
who try to tell you that Christ is here or that he is there. The destruction will certainly come. As the proverb says: "Where the car-
cass is, there will vultures be also," i.e. where there is religious and
moral decadence, there judgment will come.

The Time of the Parousia
Matthew 24.32-36

Christ said that we can get an idea as to the time of the Parousia
from the fig tree and other trees. When we see the branches becoming tender and bursting forth their leaves, then we know that
spring is coming. In the same way when you see all those things
that have been mentioned taking place you will know that the end
is coming. He assured them that all these things would happen in
their own generation. In 70 A.D. Jerusalem was destroyed and the
Gospel was preached to the then known world.

No one, however, knows the day and the hour of the Parousia
and the End. Not even the Son of Man. This remains in the absolute judgment of God the Father. Anyone trying to calculate the
exact time actually sins. He forgets that one thousand years in the
eyes of God are like one day or a few hours and moments (cf. 2
Pet. 3.8). The Parable of the Talents teaches us somehow that we
should not expect the Parousia or the kingdom of God immediately (Mt.25.14-30; Lk.19,12-27).

There are many people who attempt to acquire followers by
using threats or promises of an imminent Parousia. Christians
know that the Parousia will come and they await it vigilently, always ready by working in patience and goodness the will of God,
so that when He does come they may be found worthy of entering
into the wedding feast (Mt.24.45-52,25.1-13; Mk.13.33-37; Lk.
21.34-36). The Church steadfastly believes in the second coming
of the Lord and in the end of all things. The main purpose and
meaning of the present life is the preparation for the Parousia and
the start of a new life. We Christians live this life in Christ here
and now, but await the fulness in the Parousia, "when he comes."
The present world is becoming; it is moving toward perfection;
nothing in this world is perfect. What sort of change will actually

take place in the world we cannot know now. One thing we do know is that "a new heaven" and "a new earth" awaits us (2 Peter 3.3-13; Rev.21.1-27; Isaiah 65.17), and "we will be with the Lord forever" looking upon his glory (1 Thess.4.17; Jn.17.24).

The Parousia and the Judgment
Matthew 25.31-46

The picture of the Parousia is simple, yet alive and powerful. Christ will come as "the Son of Man," like the Jews of that time expected him to come in his heavenly glory. The dead will be resurrected and all of mankind will appear before him and will be judged (Rev.20.11-13). People were created free, and as free beings, they are responsible for their acts and their thoughts in relation to God. Each person will stand "before the tribunal of Christ" to be judged according to the good or evil done in his or her life (2 Cor.5.10). The most important criterion is the royal virtue of love. And love for our neighbor is the love of Christ who died on the cross for the life of the whole world and thus identified himself with the world. Whoever loves Christ loves also his creation—the world. Whoever does not love the world for whom Christ died does not love Christ, does not love God and for this reason he is judged.

The parable says that on that day "books will be opened and secrets will be made public." Yet before Christ we will not need to look into books. His light will penetrate our hearts and our "cardiogram" will reveal to each of us where we belong—to the right or to the left. Let us seek to do as much as possible the will of God and let us pray that his mercy will receive us at his right!

CHAPTER TWELVE

THE PASSION AND THE MYSTERY OF LOVE

The Anointing By the Woman and the Betrayal By Judas
Matthew 26.1-16; Luke 22.3-6

The time was two days before the passover feast. The high priests had already made their decision to kill Jesus. John describes the whole atmosphere and the thoughts of the leaders very strikingly (11.47-53).

According to Matthew and Mark, Jesus on this day had been invited to dinner. This dinner and the anointing are described a little differently in John. If this is the same event, does John tell us that the woman who anointed Jesus was Mary, the sister of Martha and Lazarus?

Judas left directly and agreed with the high priests to betray Jesus (Mk.13.10-11). Between the two dark images of Judas and the high priests stands the noble act of the woman, an act of great love, which was by the directive of Jesus Christ himself preserved in the Gospels for the whole world to know. From the antithesis of Judas and the myrrh-bearing woman, the Church was inspired to create those very beautiful and meaningful hymns which are sung on Holy Tuesday evening together with the remarkable hymn of Cassiani. The entire service is truly very moving for the faithful who pray during the services of Holy Week.

The Greeks Seek to See Jesus
John 12.20-23

The synoptics tell us many things which occurred between the
time of the entrance of Jesus into Jerusalem and the Last Supper.
John does not mention any of these. He does, however, record one
peculiar episode – the visitation of the Greeks. This is where it
should be taken up since it comes precisely before the Last Supper
of the Lord.

Now there were some Greeks among those who went up to worship at the feast. They came to Philip, who was from Bethsaida in
Galilee, with a request. 'Sir,' they said, 'we would like to see Jesus"
(Jn.12.20-21). These Greeks were probably proselytes who had
gone up to Jerusalem to worship. They heard for the first time
about Jesus and asked to see him, for they wanted to get to know
him. Philip and Andrew, who had Greek names, told Jesus about
them. We do not really know if Jesus received them or not, or
what he said to them, if anything. In any case, when Jesus heard
that even Greeks were seeking him, he said: "The hour has come
for the Son of Man to be glorified."

The fact that John mentions at this point the visit of the Greeks
assures us that Christ somehow connected the hour of the glory of
the cross with the coming of the Greeks. After the resurrection the
Greeks received Christ, and John, who was writing his Gospel
among the Greeks, remembered this episode and recorded it in his
Gospel. (cf. also 7.35).

After the incident with the Greeks, Jesus spoke symbolically
about his death which would bring about the fruits of faith (12.
23-26,32). The idea of his death became more fully obvious, and
Christ said "now my heart is troubled." He did not say,"My father, if it is possible, may this cup be taken from me," as he was to
say in the Garden of Gethsemane. There the cup of his Passion
was closer. Instead Jesus said:

"What shall I say? Father, save me from this hour? No, it was
for this very reason I came to this hour. Father, glorify your
name! Then a voice came from heaven,"I have glorified it and
will glorify it again" (Jn.12.27-28).

With these words Jesus accepted the cross for the salvation of the world. This is why the victorious shout follows: "Now is the time for judgment on this world; now the prince of this world will be driven out. But I, when I am lifted up from the earth, will draw all men to myself." He said this to show the kind of death he was going to die (Jn.12.31-33).

The rest is repetition and a summary by John of what Jesus generally said and of the negative stance which most of the people took toward Jesus. "Even after Jesus had done all these miraculous signs in their presence, they still did not believe in him" (Jn. 12,37). This is the bitter complaint of John throughout the whole Gospel. They did not believe! For one who has known the joy of life in Christ unbelief is a mystery. That mystery will occupy the faithful forever. John turns to Isaiah to find some sort of answer. And that is where we might all turn when we are confronted with the question of why there is unbelief (Jn.12.38-41; Mt.13.14; 4.11; Acts 28.26; Is.6.9-11,53.1). This,too,had been written. God wanted it or at least permitted it. That is the only answer. "Lord, who has believed our message?" Their hearts had grown hard; they had shut their ears and their eyes, as if they were afraid to see and believe, to repent and to be saved. This is what Isaiah said when he saw the glory of God. The glory of God which Isaiah saw was for John the glory of the Incarnate Christ. That is why he asks who can believe. To understand and believe the unfathomable mystery one needs to have an open heart, full of faith to a merciful God.

There were a few persons who did believe in the person of the messiah, but in order that they not lose their reputation they did not confess their faith, fearing that they might be ostracized from the synagogue. They preferred the glory of men rather than the glory of God.

Faith in God was, is, and always will be difficult, because repentance is difficult, the change of thoughts and purposes in life is difficult. We can all see the signs of God. Yet we want the divine to be according to our specifications and to serve us. Many times we reject the will of God, even though we see that it is good and to our benefit, simply because it comes into conflict with our own selfish pride. It is in conflict because we seek our reputation before men and do not consider our place before God. This is the mystery in the relationship between God and free man. This mystery prompted God to become man in order that he might help man rise up to God.

"Then Jesus cried out." In John 12.44-50, Christ, as if speaking from his heavenly pulpit, repeated what he had taught before: I am the light of the world, the teacher and savior sent by God; he who believes in me does not believe in me only but in the one who sent me; I have come into the world as a light, so that no one who believes in me should stay in darkness; I did not come to judge the world, but to save it; the Father who sent me commanded me what to say and how to say it. This is the eternal cry of Christ to the world which calls all of us to faith and to love, to the divine light and to life, and eternally he awaits for our response!

From this point on Christ limited himself to the narrow circle of his disciples. We are approaching the Last Supper and the Passion. The cross and the resurrection of Christ is the heart of the Christian faith. Each Evangelist sought with his own way to comprehend the whole reality. These events exceed every human thought; they are divine events, and only as such can they be approached. It is necessary to study with divine reverence all of the Gospels separately, and afterwards with the help of God, to draw for ourselves a general understanding and a complete truth about the person and the work of Christ.

The Church which has deeply and existentially lived the mystery of Christ has offered it to us as a living experience in its beautiful hymns. These hymns shed abundant light on the Mystery of Christ and enrich the services of Holy Week and the resurrection which our Church celebrates in such a remarkable way. The worship services during these days, which are rightly called great and holy days, help us a great deal to live together with the whole Church the inscrutible depth of the cross and of the resurrection.

The Preparation for the Passover Feast
Matthew 26.17-19

The first day of the Feast of Unleavened Bread for the Jews had come and Jesus sent Peter and John to "a certain man" who was familiar to them to prepare whatever was needed for the passover. At this point critical scholars struggle to determine if this day was the day of passover or the day before. The synoptics give us the impression somehow that it was the day of the Jewish passover. They "prepared the passover," but did not describe the meal as a passover meal; they make no mention of the passover lamb. John notes that this meal "was just before the passover feast." Thus Christ was crucified on the fourteenth day of Nisan, at the time when the passover lambs were being slaughtered for the Jewish passover (Ex.12,6).

If we take into account that the passover began on the evening of fourteen Nisan and that this day begins at six p.m. on thirteen Nisan, then it is possible for the disciples to say "the first day of unleavened bread" and to mean the thirteen Nisan. All the evangelists agree that the supper took place on a Thursday and the crucifixion on a Friday. On the day of crucifixion Simon was coming from the field (Mt.15,21), something which would not be taking place on the passover.

If the Last Supper took place on the eve of passover, then we can say that with the institution of the mystery of the Holy Eucharist on that evening, Christ instituted the "New Pascha."

The Last Supper

In the evening they sat for the supper. The hour was a sacred one. The betrayer had no place there. Judas either had to repent or to leave. John describes the scene in greater detail. "Jesus was troubled in spirit and testified... one of you is going to betray me" (Jn.13.21). The disciples stared at one another in amazement wondering who the traitor was and saying: "Surely not I, Lord?" Judas also said "Surely not I, Rabbi?" And Jesus answered: "Yes, it is you" (Mt.26.22,25). Peter had John who was sitting next to Jesus ask him who the traitor was, and Jesus gave him the sign: "It is the one to whom I give this piece of bread when I have dipped it in the dish." It was Judas. Jesus gave him the bread and told him: "What you are about to do, do quickly." Was Jesus in a hurry to get rid of Judas or in a hurry to quicken the time of the cross? Judas did not repent even at this last opportunity. He took the bread and left the room directly. John added: "it was night." Judas left the light and fell into darkness (13.21-30).

When Judas left the atmosphere cleared. Christ remained with his eleven disciples. Many things were said and done during that evening. Each Evangelist had recorded whatever he could and in the order he thought the best one. This is why it is necessary to study this section with greater care and with constant comparison of all the Evangelists in order to formulate as complete as possible a picture of the mystery, for indeed we have a mystery here.

The Mystery of the Holy Eucharist
Matthew 26.26-29
Mark 14.22-25; Luke 22.15-20; 1 Corinthians 11.23-26

During the course of the Last Supper Christ instituted the sacrament of the Holy Eucharist.

While they were eating, Jesus took bread, gave thanks and broke it and gave it to his disciples saying, "take and eat; this is my body."

Then he took the cup, gave thanks and offered it to them, saying "Drink from it, all of you. This is my blood of the new covenant, which is poured out for many for the forgiveness of sins. I tell you, I will not drink of this fruit of the vine from now on until that day when I drink it anew with you in my father's kingdom" (Mt.26.26-29).

The whole mystery is the seal of the new covenant which God made with mankind. With the betrayal of Judas, Christ had already accepted the cross. With his death and particularly with his blood which was poured out on the cross, a new covenant of salvation was inaugurated and sealed between God and men, in accordance with the anthology in the Old Testament where the covenant was sealed with the blood of the passover lamb (Ex.24.8; Jer.31.33-34). The blood of the Old Testament foreshadowed the blood of Christ. Christ is the true Lamb of God who bears the sin of the world. With his death the new pascha was inaugurated to transfer us to the kingdom of God (Mt.26.29; Lk.22.15-18).

Many theologians are still trying to find with the tools of logic the meaning of the words of Christ with which he instituted the Holy Eucharist. The Church, however, from the apostles to the present has known and knows that the Bread and the Wine with the blessing became precisely what Christ said—the very Body and Blood of Christ who was sacrificed for the salvation of the world. Christ preferred to remain with us in this form of the mystery as "communion" and food unto life eternal "until he comes" again, according to St. Paul (1 Cor.10.16-17, 11.23-26).

The Mystery is an experience of faith and does not stand up to rational analysis, or rather human logic does not stand up to a direct meeting with the Mystery. Our faith approaches the Mystery and worships in sacred silence. That is why this Mystery constitutes the heart of Christian worship as we live it in the Divine Liturgy.

Who is the Greatest?
Luke 22.24-27

In this most sacred moment Luke presents to us one more dark incident. While Jesus was talking about the cross the disciples were still thinking about positions of honor. This is how weak man really is! Christ, however, challenged them to take their proper place by presenting himself as "one who serves." He promised, nevertheless, that a kingdom was being prepared for those who remain faithful until the end (Lk.22.28-30).

The Last Supper
John 13-17

Here it is better to listen to John. He writes with love, with more depth, for he remembers and lives the events in the life of the Church. As we have already noted, John does not record the historical events in their exactness. Consequently, he does not tell us clearly if the Supper was a passover meal. He notes, however, that the meal took place before the passover feast. John does not even mention the institution of the Holy Eucharist. He simply presupposes that the sacraments are known to his readers. It is with these sacraments that the Church lives (3.5,6.51-58). The purpose of John is to enter more deeply into what Christ said and did and thus to reveal more fully the mystery of Christ through the Faith of the Church. For this reason John records here the farewell dis-

courses to help us also approach Christ. This is much more important than the historical accuracy of the events. None of the Evangelists thinks about historical accuracy. When someone has Christ
he does not seek accuracies; he only seeks to have his love.

For John this was indeed the last supper; it was the last night
when Christ was with his disciples. Christ knew everything that
was going to take place; the betrayal, the cross, and even the glory
which was to follow the cross. Everything he said and did is understood in the light of the cross. We could say that the words of that
evening are the theology of the cross. Christ knew that "the
hour" had come for him to go to the Father. The work for which
he became incarnate and came into the world to accomplish was
completed with the cross. Thus he could now leave the world and
return to the Father in heavenly glory (16.18). He also knew that
the Father had put everything which concerns the fortune of humanity, salvation or judgment into the hands of the Son (cf.5,22).
The love for his own reached the highest point: "He loved them to
the end." Out of love he came into the world and now he was
ready "to give up his life for his friends" (13.1-3,15.13).

Jesus Washes His Disciples Feet
John 13.4-17

Knowing all these things, Jesus "got up from the meal, took off
his outer clothing, and wrapped a towel around his waist. After
that, he poured water into a basin and began to wash his disciples
feet." St. John Chrysostom observes that Jesus probably began
with Judas. The disciples were troubled and ill at ease. Peter, as he
often did, tried to stop Jesus: "you shall never wash my feet."
Then Jesus told him: "unless I wash you you have no part with
me." With this comment Jesus gave to Peter and to all of us the
deep meaning of the symbolic act. This symbolic act is a proto-
type of the humility which he was to suffer out of his great love
for us. Humility "unto death, death on the cross," as St. Paul re-
marks. Should Peter or anyone else refuse this salutary humiliation
of his, he would not have a place with Christ, he would not enjoy
the salutary blessings which flow from the cross of Christ. Furthermore, if one does not receive the purifying power of the cross one

remains in his sins. This is the first deep meaning of the washing of the disciples' feet; this is the central idea of Christianity: the purifying power of the death of Christ. This is why John records this event.

As soon as Peter heard these words he immediately changed his mind and asked Jesus to wash not only his feet but also his hands and his head. Christ, however, reassured him. It is enough for someone to be "washed" (through faith and baptism) and he will be clean, holy.

The second meaning of the washing of the disciples's feet is the example of the teacher for the disciples (Jn.13.12-17). As human beings we always look for good examples in life. Many times we do not see this good example. We are all weak and want honors and first places (Lk.22.24f). In our thirst for an example Christ will always be the heavenly example which constantly calls us upward.

This exemplary humility of Christ was immortalized doctrinally in a very beautiful manner by St. Paul in Phil.2.6-11. Those of us who are followers of Christ must have him as our unique example for imitation precisely because we represent him in the world. Life is achieved only in the humility of the love of Christ.

The Farewell Discourses of Christ
John 13.31-17.24

During the passover meal of the Jews the father of the family reiterates the marvelous deeds of God in the past but also those deeds which are anticipated in the future in order to strengthen faith in God. Christ, too, narrated in these chapters what was expected to take place in the future. The entire section is a continuous sacred rite. He spoke about the need of separation which would take place with his death and his return to the Father. He comforted the apostles who would remain in the world, for they would not be alone. The Son and the Father and the Holy Spirit would be with them. Finally, Christ encompassed everyone in his prayer to the Father.

The Hour of Glory As the Hour of Separation
John 13.31-14.11

"When he (Judas) was gone, Jesus said, 'Now is the Son of Man glorified and God is glorified in him'" (Jn.13.31). This phrase gives us the whole atmosphere of this mystical initiation of the apostles. The Christ who spoke was already the Christ of glory. This hour was the hour of glory about which he had spoken so often before. It was the hour of glory because it was the hour of the cross. The cross was the glory of the Son but also the glory of the Father. The cross was the will of God for the salvation of the world. With the cross Christ completed the work which the Father had given him to do; the world was saved; the will of God triumphed, and the Father was glorified in the Son. But the Father also glorified the Son and made him "Lord of all" (Phil.2.8-11). When John was recording these discourses for us, the Church was already living in this glory of the Father and of the Son.

The Hour of Separation
John 13.33-14.31

"My children, I will be with you only a little longer. You will look for me, and just as I told the Jews, so I tell you now: Where I am going, you cannot come" (Jn. 13.33).

The hour of separation had come and Jesus announced it tenderly to His disciples. Soon in the persons of Judas and the Jewish leaders, the "ruler of this world" would come to lead Jesus to the cross. The disciples did not know very well the reality of this separation, but who can? They were still thinking in terms of this world, about a struggle against the opponents. Peter promised that he was ready to follow Christ and even to give his life for Him. Christ, however, predicted that Peter would deny Him three times before the rooster crowed. These words of Christ sounded harsh. The disciples were now troubled not only over the separation but also because it was possible that they, too, might deny Him. They had already experienced what happened to Judas who was one of the twelve.

Man is always afraid when he finds himself alone in life, separated from Christ, without hope and without God in the world. Even today when we are overwhelmed by the abundance of good things, the agony of life becomes greater without Christ.

Jesus reassured His disciples: "Do not let your hearts be troubled. Trust in God; trust also in me" (Jn. 14.1). The only thing needed in this difficult time is faith. Faith in God and in Christ overcomes any trouble; it overcomes the world which causes this trouble! Separation does not mean we have failed. The cross is not defeat but victory. Through the cross I have completed my work and return to the Father as victor. There I shall prepare a place for you and will return to take you there with me—"to be with me where I am" (Jn. 14.1-3, 17.24).

The phrases: "I am going to the father"; "In my father's house are many rooms"; "I shall not leave you orphans"; "I shall come again to take you with me" are eschatological expressions familiar to the people of that time. They introduce us to the deeper understanding of the mystery of the person and work of Christ, who came from heaven to raise the world with Himself and to bring it back to heaven from whence it fell. This is the cycle of Christ. From the Father He came down to earth to rise again "to where he was before" and not to remain on earth.

Christ came from the Father and returned to the Father (Jn. 16.5). The disciples, too, will go to the Father. This is the life purpose of all of us. But which is the way toward the Father, toward God?

"I Am the Way and The Truth and The Life"
John 14.16

Truth in religious and philosophical language is that absolute reality which embraces in itself everything; truth is God Himself where true life is to be found. This divine reality and this true life man has seen only in the person of Christ. Christ is not one of the teachers of truth. In Christ we meet truth itself, that divine reality which gives life to the world. To approach God it is first necessary to approach, to know and to be united to Christ. United with Christ, we continually go to the Father. "No one comes to the Father except through me." Christ is the only direct way which surely leads to the Father. Thus Christ is the goal of our life because He is the way which leads us to God.

"Philip said, 'Lord show us the Father and that will be enough for us.' Jesus said to him . . . Anyone who has seen me has seen the Father." (Jn.14.8-9). Christ is the visible image of the invisible God. Whoever knows Christ well has already come to know the Father, the source of life. In the person of Christ we meet God, we are united with the Father and have life (Jn.14.7-11; Col.1.15-17).

The New Life in Christ
John 14.12-31

Be not afraid therefore. I go as victor to the Father and thus I inaugurate a new condition of life for the world. In this new condition of life you will ask in my name and I, being present with you, will do what you ask for the glory of God (Jn. 14.12-14). That which is required of you is to love me and to obey my commandments, especially the great commandment to love. This love will be the distinguishing mark that you belong to me (Jn. 13.34-35). Without love you are not mine and you cannot ask nor receive. "If you love me," I will ask the Father to send the Holy Spirit Who will remain with you forever. He will be the other counselor in my place. He will be the comforter, the enabler, and the defender at the difficult times of your life. He will guide you to the whole truth; He will help you to understand better the mystery of the cross and the new condition of life created by the cross.

"I will not leave you as orphans." Do not be so discouraged. I will not leave you alone in your life. Not only the Holy Spirit will be with you but I myself—"I will come to you." You will see me again soon. "Because I live, you will also live," and know that "I am in you."

"On that day" of the new life and of the presence of the Holy Spirit, you will really understand the divine bond which unites us all in a perfect unity. Then you, too, will realize that "I am in my Father, and you are in me, and I am in you." This happens because he who loves me and obeys my commandments is loved by my Father and we shall come to dwell in Him as friends forever (Jn. 14.18-24).

These things I have been able to tell you as long as I am still with you. The rest you will hear from the Holy Spirit. And now "Peace I leave with you; my peace I give you." The peace I give you is certain because it is grounded in my relationship with the Father and it unites you also with the Father. "Do not let your hearts be troubled and do not be afraid." If you really loved me as you should, and if you only knew the joy I feel as I am going to the Father, you, too, would rejoice instead of being sad. "I am going to the Father for the Father is greater than I." He is the original source of all. He holds and governs. He also directs the work of salvation and from Him come all the blessings.

The prince of this world is coming. In the persons of the leaders he will make his last attack! However, he will not find any sin in me in order to claim me as his own. I am going to the cross simply because I want the world to learn that "I love the Father and I do exactly what my Father has commanded me."

"Come now; let us leave." I am going to meet the enemy (Jn. 14.31; cf. 13.27).

Christ the True Vine
John 15.1-8

Christ tried to comfort His disciples by promising them that He would be with them again. He wanted to leave for Gethsemane, but the disciples remained motionless. The though of separation was unbearable and sadness heavily marked their faces. They could not understand the depth of the cross and its consequences for the Church. Thus Jesus continued to speak to them a little longer. Possibly they were standing up as Jesus continued to speak. He repeated first the same things, but somehow more clearly. Christ saw the apostles as the Church which would remain behind in the world to continue the work of salvation. He foresaw the hatred of the world against them, and in order to comfort them he emphasized the close relationship they have in a mutual koinonia (fellowship) of love. The Father, the Son, and the Holy Spirit will be together in the single work of salvation, for it is the work of God.

"I am the true vine and my Father is the gardener. He cuts off every branch in me that bears no fruit, while every branch that does bear fruit he trims clean so that it will be even more fruitful" (Jn.15.1-2).

In the Old Testament the vine was the symbol for the people of God (Is.5.1-7; Mt.21.33-41). Unfortunately, it did not bear the fruits of faith and love which God expected. Christ and the Church now have taken the place of the people of God. Christ is the true vine as God wanted it. The apostles, the Christians are the branches of the vine. This image of the vine shows how organically united into one are the disciples and Christ, just as the vine branches are united to the trunk and the roots. Christ alone is the true Israel. He alone incarnates in himself the people of God. He is the whole Church. We are the branches. Our entire spiritual life and spiritual fruitfulness depends absolutely upon this union. This is a guarantee for the success of our work but also a strong exhortation for all of us to remain always united with Christ. Otherwise failure and judgment are certain.

"Abide in me, and I in you. As the branch cannot bear fruit by itself; unless it abides in the vine, neither can you, unless you abide in me" (Jn.25.4f).

"Abide in My Love," remain in my love as I remain in the love of the Father. Divine love is the atmosphere in which the faithful breathe. It is love of the stature and the style of the love which Christ has for the Father, and it is love in the measure of the love of the Holy Trinity (Jn.15.9-17).

Friends of Christ
John 15.13-18

Greater love has no one than this, that he lay down his life for his friends. You are my friends if you do what I command.

Friendship is the most valuable thing in a person's life. Christ calls us his friends. The greatest honor a person can receive is to be called a "friend of God." This honor, however, is given not as if we were equal to him" but because Christ called us out of love and made us his friends. Christ made us communicants in the mysteries of God unto salvation, he who is in the Father's bosom and has learned everything from the Father (cf.Jn.1.18,15.15). A Christian, of course, must never forget the creature-creator distance between man and God. Our relation is a relation of worship.

"This is my command: Love each other" (Jn.15.17). Christ said all these things to teach us to live with love. Faith, love, prayer, communion with Christ and the Father and the Holy Spirit—these are the life of the Church. Above all, there is love. This is the new commandment, and the only one which encompasses all the other commandments yet adds its own special flavor to them (Jn.13. 34-35). Love will be the main characteristic of the disciples of Christ. Love is the fulfilment of the law (Rom.13.10).

The Church in the World
John 15.18-16.4

The world of creation is not evil; it is the creation of God. But because of Adam's fall, the world has revolted and stands in opposition to the salutary will of God. Love is to reign in the Church, but in the world, which has not accepted the love of Christ, there is hatred. Only Christ and God are love. The world has hated Christ and it will also hate the Church which bears the truth about salvation in Christ. This should not seem strange to us. Only when the Church becomes worldly, when it, too, becomes "the world," only then will the world not hate it (Jn.15.18-19). People hate the Church because they do not know Christ. They live as if Christ has not come. Without Christ, man cannot know God who sent him. Christ came and taught the people and did great works and signs "which no one else has ever done." "They have seen and they have hated both me and my Father." This is the one great, unjustifiable and inexplicable sin of unbelief. The only explanation for the believer of this unbelief is that this, too, is mentioned in the Scriptures—"They hated me without reason" (Ps.34.19,69.4).

With these words John indicates that the believers do not belong to the world. "I have chosen you out of the world. That is why the world hates you." The question really is to what extent we as believers demonstrate with our lives that we are different, indeed select, that we have known Christ and have truly acknowledged him as Lord and ruler of our lives (Phil. 2.6-11).

The Other Counselor
John 16.5-15

"Now I am going to him who sent me." Christ came from eternity and to eternity he returned (Jn.1.1,14; 13.3; 17.8). This is how the disciples had to understand the separation. The disciples, however, instead of feeling joy and asking what Christ would send them from the Father, were actually filled with grief in their hearts. Christ had to go back to the Father in order to send the Holy Spirit, who would continue the work of Christ in the Church. There were many things more which Christ had to tell his disciples about himself, about his work, about their work in the world, but the disciples could not bear to hear it and could not understand it. "When he, the Spirit of truth comes, he will guide you in all truth" (Jn.16.13). The Holy Spirit is the "other Counselor" who has come in the place of Christ. He will bear witness to me and together with him, you, too, will bear witness, Christ said. Thus throughout the Church the work of Christ would be continued in the world (Jn.15.22-27,16.7-15).

The Separation

The hour of the final separation had come. In "a little while, and you will not see me, and again a little while, and you will see me" (Jn.16.17). Jesus meant he was going to the Father through the cross. The world of unbelief would rejoice thinking that is has won. You will be sorrowful, but your sorrow will turn to joy" (Jn. 16.21). A woman giving birth to a child has pain because her time has come; but when her baby is born she forgets the anguish because of her joy that a child is born into the world. So with you: Now is your time of grief, but I will see you again and you will rejoice, and no one will take your joy from you because a new day and a new age will begin—a new creation will begin with the cross (cf.Jn.16.16-22). In that new day you will no longer ask me anything. You will ask of the Father and he will give you whatever you need for your work and for your life. That will be the day and age of the ineffable joy which will not be taken away. Ask therefore in my name and you will receive and your joy will be complete and perfect (cf.Jn.16.23-24). These things which I tell you are like parables, you cannot understand the entire depth of their richness. On that day, however, I will speak to you clearly about the Father and our relationship. Then you will understand that the Father loves you because you have loved me and "have believed that I came from God." (Jn.16.25-28).

This is the theme of John: Christ is the one sent by the Father and what he says and what he does are words and deeds of the Father. The disciples finally thought they understood him and confessed the faith: "you came from God." Jesus accepted the confession, yet he also knew human weakness, and predicted they would abandon him. But he was not alone. Even on the cross the Father was with him. Thus, the discourses ended on a note of triumph:

I have told you these things, so that in me you may have peace. In this world you will have trouble. But take heart! I have overcome the world" (Jn.16.33).

The end would not be the scandal of the cross, but the victory of the cross. Through the cross the world of sin, of unbelief and of hatred was overcome and judged (Jn.12.31). The world lost the game it tried to play with Christ when it raised him on the cross.

The victory of Christ with the cross and the resurrection was an eschatological event; it referred to the end and ultimate purpose of the world. Indeed it has universal significance for all time; it is a victory for the whole world. The victory of Christ is the counterpart of the defeat of Adam. Whatever was destroyed by Adam was restored by Christ through the obedience of the cross (Rom.5.12-21). The victory of Christ became the victory of the Church. "This is the victory that has overcome the world, even our faith" (1 Jn.5.4). It is remarkable to note that St. John was writing this when both he and the Church were being persecuted by the Romans!

The High Priestly Prayer
John 17.1-26

With the words in ch.13-16 John brings us to the summit. The disciples could not endure anymore. Nothing remained to be said than the prayer which would sanctify everything that had been said. It is a prayer in dialogue between the Son and the Father in a language that only they understand, and in which the Holy Spirit will teach believers about the love of God and the glory which awaits us together with Christ.

It is a prayer of doxology for the work which has been completed (Jn.17.1-5). The glory is mutual because the will and the work are mutually the Son's and the Father's. The Son revealed the name of the Father to mankind. Through Christ we have a new knowledge of God which gives life eternal, which saves the world (Jn.17.2-3). This was the purpose of the Incarnation. Without Christ there would be no knowledge of God. Without knowledge of God man doesn't have real life. This is the glory of the Son which makes him one with the Father, for in the Son we have seen the Father and have life eternal.

Now that the Son is leaving, his prayer is for the Church which will continue to make God known in the world.

In the prayer of the Son to the Father we see the very heart of God throbbing with love for his children for those who have believed and for those who will believe in Christ (17.6-11,20-26; Rom.8.34). God is love, and his love embraces us all.

"Protect them by the power of your name." The name of God is Jahveh, the One Who Is, indicating the inscrutible nature of God. In Christ, however, God appeared as Divine Love in action for the salvation of his world (Jn.3.16). Protect them by the power of your name means: continue to keep them united in your love as I have kept them until now united in your love.

"Sanctify Them by Thy Truth"
John 17.17-19

The purpose of the Church is the sanctification of the world: to present the world "holy and sinless" before the Holy God. This can only happen with our faith and participation in the Truth. Truth is whatever God says to us in Christ (Heb.1.1-2). Christ came to earth as the Truth which sanctifies. He is the "Holy One of God, whom the Father sanctified and sent to the world." By his death on the cross Christ sanctified himself for our sake; as he sanctifies us as the great High Priest, he offered himself to sanctify us (Jn.10.36,17.19). The Truth of Christ is a new spiritual atmos-

phere of divine grace which Christ inaugurated and which the believers can breathe. They are sanctified by participating in his holiness, his sacrifice. The Church itself is sanctified and in the Church
the world is constantly sanctified in the Holy Spirit until the
whole world becomes Church, i.e., God's world. Thus the prayer
"Sanctify them by thy truth" seeks to keep the disciples steadfast
in their faith and life in Christ.

The Unity of the Church
John 17.21-23

In the high priestly prayer Christ prayed not only for those present, but also for all those future believers in the gospel of the
Church so that all may be united as one—as the Father and the
Son are one. "I in them and you in me," so that there may be perfect unity. Through our union with Christ we are also united with
the Father and have life eternal. This is the glory which Christ has
brought us. Only in such unity of the Church in Christ can the
"world" know and believe that the Father sent the Son and that
He loves the world as much as he loved the Son. Thus the world
can be saved and become the people and the kingdom of God.

The Prayer for Perfection
John 17.24-26

The prayer here opens up toward the eschatological events. It
embraces the entire divine plan for the world from before the creation of the world to even beyond the bounds of history at the end
of the world and into eternity. He wants all of us to be with him.
The will of the Son is also the will of the Father. Thus what the
Son seeks to do is the will of God and as the will of God it will
certainly become reality (cf.Jn.5.19-30).

"Father, I want those you have given me to be with me where I
am" (Jn.17.24). In the existence of the Son there is no past and
future. The Son exists and acts within an eternal present. In this
eternal present the believers also live within the eternal love of the
Father and the Son. They enjoy the Son's glory in its eternity: the

glory which the Son had from before the beginning of the world, the glory which "we have seen" at the Incarnation (Jn.1.14), the glory we experience in the life of his Church, and finally the glory which we shall be seeing after the end of the world when we shall be with him in eternity (Jn.17.24-26; 1 Thess.4.17).

> I have made you known to them, and will continue to make you known in order that the love you have for me may be in them and that I myself may be in them (Jn.17.26).

The disciples came to know God and Christ in his life and teachings. They were to come to know more of him on the cross and in the resurrection. And they continue to know him forever through the Holy Spirit in the Church in order to live in the divine love of the Father and the Son.

This is the glory, the joy and the blessedness of the true Christians. The perfection of this glory will come to pass. It is toward this perfection that we are constantly moving with nostalgia—to see the glory of God which we shall never be able to experience in its fullness in this present life. There, in the end, the love of God will meet with the justice of God (Jn.17.25).

The prayer says "protect them," "sanctify them," and "keep them in perfect unity" (Jn.17.11,17,23). The worship accomplishes all these, particularly in the divine liturgy as it was formulated in Byzantium.

This is the dialectic between God and the world, which John so marvelously presents to us in his gospel. The world needs to be fulfilled, perfected, with the help of God, but this must be done freely. That is why God became man in order to help man become divine. This is why the Church does not leave the world but with its life in Christ and with prayer seeks to change the world, to give it a new "knowledge of itself" in the love of God in Christ. For this reason we should all pray the prayer of Christ.

The Agony of Gethsemane
Matthew 26.36-46; Luke 22.40-46; John 18.1-11

When he had finished praying, Jesus left with his disciples and crossed the Kidron Valley. On the other side there was an olive grove, and he and his disciples went into it (Jn. 18.1).

After the mystical initiation of the disciples, the high-priestly prayer to the Father and the singing of the hymns, Jesus went to the Mount of Olives in the town of Gethsemane.

It is at this point that the Synoptics placed the prediction about the temptation of Peter (Lk. 22.31-34; Mt. 26.27-35). From here on Jesus moves directly to the betrayal and to the cross—the glory of Jesus.

Jesus left the eight disciples a little behind, and went ahead with the three. These three disciples were closer to Jesus; he had taken the same three to Mount Tabor where they were witnesses of the glory of his tranfiguration.

Now Jesus "began to be sorrowful and troubled," and said to his disciples: "My soul is very sorrowful even to death" (Mt.26.37-38). It was the hour of the cup of the cross before which Christ himself was perplexed. Why this cup? Why so much sin? Why so much unrepentance in the world that led him now to the cross? Why had death entered abnormally into God's world? And above all, why was it necessary to overcome sin and death with the suffering of the Righteous One? Simple logic will never be able to respond to these ultimate questions. Revelation simply says "it is necessary for Christ to suffer." Only faith and prayer—only communion with the Father—can throw some light on the mystery.

"Stay here and keep watch with me." His soul was deeply grieved. He then left the three disciples and went to pray alone. Many times prayer has secrets which are very personal, and one seeks to be alone, to speak personally with God, even when one finds himself in a crowd. In such circumstances the many cannot help. The soul struggles alone in prayer, while faith and love for God are tested and strengthened.

Going a little further, he fell to the gound and prayed that if possible the hour might pass from him. "Father," he said, "everything is possible for you. Take this cup from me. Yet not what I will, but what you will" (Mk.14.36).

It is very difficult for anyone to comment on these words. Only on our knees in prayer and spiritual awe before the great mystery can we read and meditate on this passage. Jesus struggled on his knees with prayer to the Father. Three times he prayed for the same thing: Why the cross for salvation? "My Father, if it is possible, may this cup be taken from me. Yet not as I will, but as you will" (Mt.26.39). It is to do your will that I have come to this hour (Jn.12.27).

The Father did not respond to the prayer in the way the Son, humanly speaking, would have preferred; he did not recall the "cup." The Son, however, realized once again that the cross was indeed the will of the Father. Salvation would be accomplished only with the self-sacrificing love of the Son and never with power and force. This was sufficient answer to the prayer. Luke adds that an angel appeared to strengthen him in the struggle of his prayer. "His sweat was like drops of blood falling to the ground," as if he wanted to sanctify it too (Lk.22.43).

After the prayer Jesus proceeded deliberately to offer his life for the sheep. He returned to the disciples and found them asleep, exhausted from sorrow. Peter could not remain awake even an hour for his teacher! Jesus understood them and that was why he counseled them. "Watch and pray so that you will not fall into temptation. The spirit is willing, but the body is weak" (Mt.26.41). Man is weak, and without the divine grace of prayer he falls into temptation. Christ has had experience of temptations and he can help those who are tempted (Mt.4.16; Heb.2.18). That is why he taught us to pray: "lead us not into temptation, but deliver us from the evil one."

CHAPTER THIRTEEN

THE BETRAYAL, TRIAL AND CRUCIFIXION

The Evangelists describe the dark scene of the betrayal vividly; they understand it: "Judas, one of the twelve, arrived," and with him came a large crowd armed with swords and clubs along with a few of the leaders of the people. They came at night to arrest Jesus as if he were a common thief. They were "sons of darkness" and only there in the darkness could their power be demonstrated.

With a false kiss Judas betrayed the teacher. Peter became angry and pulled out his sword. But Christ who knows all things told him: "Put your sword away." The cup of the cross is given by the Father and I must drink it. "And he touched the man's ear and healed it" (Lk.22.51; Jn.18.10-11). Jesus had also spoken before to his disciples about the cup of the cross but they had not understood him. Peter always wanted to protect Jesus. The sinister scene of the kiss by Judas is not related by John. In John Jesus appeared to the attackers with a magnificent bearing and as the good shepherd that he is, he seeks to protect his disciples from the wolves.

"Who is it you want?" Jesus asked. "Jesus of Nazareth," they replied. "I am he....If you are looking for me, then let these men go" (Jn.18.4-9). And indeed the disciples did leave. Only John who knew the high priest followed the crowd. Peter, too, followed, but secretly and from afar. Mark does not mention John in the courtyard of the high priest. He writes the 'Gospel' of Peter and speaks only of Peter. John, however, writes like an eyewitness. In any case neither Peter nor John, who remained close to Jesus, could offer him something at the time. The mystery of the cross was the will of God and did not depend upon people. Jesus gave himself up and no one could help him. After the cross and the resurrection, the disciples would need to bear witness and if need be to die for Christ. And they were witnesses and they did die for Christ.

The Trial of Jesus
Matthew 26.57-75; Luke 22.54-71; John 18.12-27

The guard of soldiers that was with the crowd and the leaders seized Jesus and took him to the home of the archpriest Caiaphas. There the hypocritical questioning took place. The decision to kill him had already been made. According to St. John, a preliminary investigation was made by Annas, the father-in-law of Caiaphas (18.12-23). During this investigation, the magnificance of Christ was revealed, while the smallness of the archpriest and his cohorts was uncovered.

The leaders sought to obtain false testimony to justify the condemnation of Jesus to death, but were not successful (Mt.26.59-61). Finally, the archpriest Caiaphas became impatient and directly posed the crucial question to Jesus: "I charge you under oath by the living God: 'Tell us if you are the Christ, the Son of God.' 'Yes, it is as you say,' Jesus replied." According to Luke, Jesus replied as follows:

> If I tell you, you will not believe me, and if I asked you to tell me what you really believe about me, you would not answer. But from now on, the Son of Man will be seated at the right hand of the mighty God. (Lk.22.68-69).

The archpriest asked Jesus under oath and Jesus answered him indirectly: your own mouth said that I am the Christ. You do not believe me and yet very soon you will see the Christ sitting victoriously at the right hand of God and he will come as judge of the world, as the prophet Daniel had foreseen (7.13). Then the archpriest very indignantly tore his clothes and said: "He has spoken blasphemy! Why do we need any more witnesses? Look, now you have heard the blasphemy. What do you think?" "He is worthy of death," they answered (Mt.26.65-66). This was what they wanted and this was what they achieved: they found the excuse to condemn the innocent one to death. From a corrupt opinion a corrupt decision was reached. One often wonders: did all those present agree on the verdict? Was Nicodemos present? Why did he not speak? And if he did speak, what could he have done? The appropriate leaders had made their decision and had taken the necessary steps to have the majority vote required by the Law. Everything was done legally, but everything that is legal is not necessarily also just.

After Jesus was condemned by the great leaders, the crowd had the opportunity to demonstrate its own meanness. It was during this scene that Peter appeared. He was forced by the circumstances to deny Christ three times, just as Jesus had foretold. Why did the always impetuous Peter deny Christ before the crowd? Was it out of fear for himself or so that he would not be expelled from the courtyard? We shall never know. The rooster crowed, Christ saw Peter, and Peter "went outside and wept bitterly" (Lk.22.62; Mt. 26.67-75). Let us pray that we may not find ourselves in such a difficult situation where we shall be forced to deny Christ, for it is very easy to forget him in our relations with the world. Forgetting him is a form of denial.

In the morning the Sanhedrin issued the formal decision condemning Jesus to death. They tied Christ as if he were a criminal, and they took him to Pilate, who was the only authorized official to execute the punishment of death. Death of the innocent one was the "righteousness" sought by the defenders of the Mosaic Law (Mt.27.1-2; Lk.23.1).

The Fate of Judas
Matthew 27.3-10; Acts I.18

In the meantime when Judas saw that Jesus was condemned to death, he was overcome by remorse for his act of betrayal. Did he not expect it? He returned the money saying, "I have sinned, For I have betrayed innocent blood." Judas threw the money into the temple and left. He went away and hanged himself. He acknowledged the fact that he had sinned, but he did not shed the tears of repentance as Peter did. He remained without Christ, and life without Christ has no meaning; it was unbearable and he committed suicide.

Through the words of Judas the high priests heard once again that they condemned an innocent man. This, too, was a challenge to repentance. It remained unheeded. The leaders tried to hide behind the traitor saying: "What is that to us? That's your responsibility." Here, too, they wanted to come out innocent: Adam once said: "It was Eve who deceived me." The thirty pieces of silver were used to purchase a burial place for foreigners, probably migrant pilgrims. Thus, as if innocent of any wrongdoing, the leaders then proceeded to Pilate to ask him to execute the death penalty upon Jesus of Nazareth.

Jesus Before Pilate
John 18.28-19.16; Luke 23.2-5

The leaders took Jesus to Pilate. They remained outside the palace "to avoid ceremonial uncleanness," as John rather ironically notes. They condemned to death the only righteous person, but had moral scruples about entering the courtyard of a gentile! Such is the morality of the letter of the law which can never touch the heart.

Pilate attempted to avoid this unjust trial, but the leaders insisted, accusing Christ as a criminal deserving the death penalty, which only Pilate could order. John notes that this was happening to fulfill the word of Jesus who had said that he would die on the cross (3.14,12.33,18.28-32). Wishing to irritate Pilate, the leaders accused Jesus of being a political revolutionary, teaching the people not to pay taxes to Caesar and proclaiming himself Messiah-king (Lk.23.2-5).

Later, "Pilate then went back inside the palace, summoned Jesus and asked him, "are you the king of the Jews?" Jesus replied with a question: "Is that your own idea or did others talk to you about me?" In any case you should know that "my kingdom is not of this world...my kingdom is from another place," and does not depend on the powers of this world. "You are a king, then!" retorted the startled Pilate. Jesus replied, "You are right in saying I am a king." But I am a different kind of king. "In fact, for this reason I was born, and for this reason I came into the world, to testify to the truth," to teach and to present to the world the truth about God and about man. This is my royal authority.Those who hear me and love the truth believe and become members of the kingdom of truth.

People have always thirsted for the truth. The entire effort of the philosophers, the endless meditation on man, seeks to know the truth, the truth seen in the world and in the mind hidden behind the beautiful world. The philosophers always acknowledged and confessed that the truth in itself and in its entirety is a mystery inaccessible to the natural mind of man. The beauty, harmony and grandeur of the physical world always directs us beyond the world to find its source and its meaning; they are signs leading us to a creator God. Only Christ came from above to testify to the truth. He himself is the truth. He is in the bosom of the Father and can speak to us about God and about man and can shed light upon the ultimate questions of life. This is the essence of the mystery of Christianity, the revelation of divine truth. In Christ we have the incarnation of truth. "Grace and truth came through Jesus Christ," and became known to us as divine reality. In Christ we know God and man in his relation to God, and therin is life eternal (Jn.17.2-3). One must thirst for truth and be on the side of truth in order to hear it, to receive it and to make it the rule in one's life. The many, like Pilate, are not moved by the truth. When challenged to decide about the truth they escape with an indifferent grimace and "what is truth?" Christ, of course, does not respond to such indifference and man remains in darkness. This is the complaint of John who particularly emphasizes the truth he saw in the person of Christ (1.5-18, 8.45-47, 14.6).

After this dialogue with Jesus Pilate declared to the Jews that he found "no basis for a charge against him." He attempted to set him free by grace of the passover feast. But the crowd was misguided by the leaders and demanded that grace be given to Barabbas the robber rather than to Jesus, the king of the Jews who was to be crucified!

Usually people are good, and when they have good leaders they can do wonders. But when the leaders are corrupt, the people can destroy everything. This is the reason for the great responsibility which leaders bear before God.

At this point we can mention in parenthesis the incident of Pilate's wife which made him more careful with Jesus(Mt.27.12-20), and perhaps made him send Jesus to Herod (Lk.23.1-6).

Pilate made one more effort to avoid the great responsibility of executing Jesus. He turned Jesus over to his soldiers to scourge him. The soldiers mockingly dressed him with a royal robe and ridiculed him. Pilate once again came out to the people and declared that he found no basis for a charge against him. He presented Jesus clothed in a purple robe and wearing a crown of thorns. "Here is the man!" he said. The chief priests and their officials shouted "Crucify! Crucify!.. he must die, because he claimed to be the Son of God" (Jn.19.6-7). John saw in Jesus the *Man,* the image of God, the king, the Son of God, then he described everything so clearly.

When Pilate heard that Jesus was the Son of God he was afraid, and going back inside the palace asked Jesus, "Where do you come from?" Are you really from heaven? The question was not one of faith, a sincere question, and Jesus again remained silent. No one can receive the answer to this great question when the question itself is not asked out of faith, when it is not an existential question for the one who asks it. Only real faith can understand Christ as the truth that contains all and gives meaning to all.

Now more than before Pilate wanted to release Jesus. He was indeed afraid! The leaders, however, mustered all the support they could and changed the accusation from a religious one to a political one, which they shouted very forcefully: "If you let this man go, you are no friend of Caesar. Anyone who claims to be a king opposes Caesar" (Jn.19.12). There is the meanness of evil. Pilate was beaten; he could no longer hide behind his indifference and neutrality. He was afraid of the leaders and of the crowd. Once again he took Jesus out to the Jews and said, "Here is your king." Unknowingly, he prophesied that Jesus of Nazareth is the king of the Jews. Finally, "wanting to satisfy the crowd, Pilate released Barabbas to them...and handed Jesus over to be crucified" (Mk. 15.15). The only thing remaining for Pilate to do was to wash his hands, while the people took upon themselves the responsibility of the sin:"Let this blood be on us and on our children!" (Mt.27.25).

John observed the events of the crucifixion with agonizing pain and described the place and the hour of the crucifixion which was about noon.

The trial of Jesus was essentially the trial of the Jewish leaders and even more generally the trial of the world of unbelief. The religious leaders of Israel, and Pilate as the political leader, represented the world. The leaders of Israel gambled everything to achieve their sinister goal. Evil made them betray all of their religious and moral principles. They admitted the hated Caesar as their king and thus denied the anticipated messiah-king: "We have no king but Caesar" (Jn.19.26). After the high priests came Pilate. He found himself before Christ who is the heavenly truth and king, who came to raise up the people and the leaders. If Pilate had only accepted the truth, he would have been the first Christian ruler in the world. He tried to remain neutral, indifferent to the truth. The one responsible for justice denied responsibility. In the end, he was forced by fear and the crowd to condemn Jesus to death against his own conscience. This is how man will always fall as long as he refuses to take his proper position before the truth, before Christ, and before God.

On the Way to Golgotha
John. 19.17-24

With the condemnatory decision of Pilate, Christ with the cross on his shoulder moved toward Golgotha. On the way they found "a certain man from Cyrene, Simon, the father of Alexander and Rufus, who was passing by on his way in from the country, and they forced him to carry the cross" (Mk.15.21; Mt.27.32; Rom. 16.13).

The women were grieving for Christ but he told them not to cry for him but for themselves, for their children and for the destruction which would befall the nation (Lk.23.26-32). The destruction of Jerusalem in 70 A.D. was indeed a great calamity.

The procession reached Golgotha. "There they crucified him, along with the criminals—one on his right, the other on his left" (Lk.23.33). An inscription was placed on the cross. It read, "Jesus of Nazareth, the King of the Jews." It was written in Greek Aramaic and Latin so that everyone could read it. The Jews protested to Pilate about this inscription, but what was already written remained, as a prophecy, since Jesus who was crucified for us is the messiah-king and savior of the world.

The scene of the crucifixion was both fearsome and didactic. Christ was raised and "Hung on the wood of the cross." The soldiers below divided his garments among themselves. John saw the seamless robe of Christ and envisioned him as the great high-priest and eternal mediator between God and mankind. That is why John mentions this seamless garment separately (Jn.19.23-24).

The faceless crowd continued to revile Jesus even on the cross and thus once again demonstrated its pettiness. On the dark side of the cross looms indifference, contempt, hatred, and evil. On the other side, however, the cross shines forth the light of Christ. On the cross Christ was praying and Luke has saved for us a couple of his words: "Father, forgive them, for they do not know what they are doing" (Lk.23.34). His agony for our salvation was greater than the pain of the cross! This prayer contains the whole meaning of the incarnation and of the cross. Christ became man and died on the cross as an eternal high-priestly messiah of God for our sins. During his entire life he did nothing but call the world to repentance to be forgiven and saved. With the sacrifice on the cross, forgiveness became an eternal reality for all mankind. This was why even then on the cross he prayed for those who were around the cross but also for the entire world. Undoubtedly the prayer of Christ helped the repentent robber to turn to Christ with faith and to say: "Jesus, remember me when you come into your kingdom" (Lk.23.42-43). Similarly, Christ's prayer helped Nicodemos and Joseph to openly become disciples of Christ, and the centurian to believe and to confess: "Surely, this man was the Son of God" (Mk.15.39).

The Mother of Jesus and the Disciple Whom Jesus Loved
John 19.25-27

During his earthly ministry, Christ gave us on one occasion reason to believe that he did not think so much about his mother (cf. Jn.2.4; Mk.3.31-35). And yet at the difficult moment on the cross Christ took particular care to provide for his mother. He placed her under the protection of his beloved disciple John, who records this detail in his gospel. This act is one more proof that the Virgin Mary, as sacred tradition has always believed, did not have any other natural children.

The Depth of the Cross
Matthew 27.45-50

About the ninth hour Jesus cried out in a loud voice, *"Eloi, Eloi, lama sabach-thani?"* which means, "My God, my God, why have you forsaken me?" (Mt.27.46). The thought of man ceases at the shout of *"Eloi, Eloi,"* The mind of man shudders at the sound of "Why have you forsaken me?" The words could possibly derive from Psalm 22, where we also find the quotation "They divided my garments among themselves." The citation of the psalm was only natural and does not subtract anything from the reality of the agonizing sorrow which Christ felt and chose to express somewhat loudly with the phrases from Psalm 22. The cross of Christ, which was the darkest sin that fallen man could ever commit, was also the cruelest form of punishment. On the cross Christ experienced all of the psychic pain and psychic darkness which was the guilt of sin of all the people. This was clearly foretold by the prophet Isaiah in 53.5-6:

> He was pierced for our transgressions, he was crushed for our iniquities; the punishment that brought us peace was upon him, and by his wounds we are healed. We all, like sheep, have gone astray, each of us has turned to his own way; and the Lord has laid on him the iniquity of us all.

This is why the cross appeared as if it were an abandonment by God; as if it were a curse and the wrath of God. This then explains the shout, "My God, my God, why have you forsaken me?" In this shout, the divine mystery of salvation in Christ was revealed to us in action. Here the mystery of salvation in Christ was carried out: "It is finished." The work of salvation was fulfilled with the passion of the savior. The resurrection would be the manifestation and confirmation of the mystery. According to the Christian faith the phrase, "Why have you forsaken me?" is understood as a ques-

tion. My God, my God, for what purpose, for what reason did salvation need to be accomplished through the cross? God never really abandoned Christ. Even on the cross Christ said *my* God; he still
spoke to God the Father. God was always with Christ. He did the
works of salvation in Christ. God the Father was closer than ever
before to Christ on the cross, saving his world. This was how Isaiah
foresaw the savior messiah—as a sacrificial lamb bearing the sin of
the world. He took up our iniquities and suffered for our sins (Is.
53.4-11; Jn.1.29). Christ died on the cross by taking our place
there, by taking upon himself the sins of everyone. This was how
Paul saw him also (2Cor.5.19-21). This was the meaning of the
phrases at the last supper: "This is my body which is broken for
you...This is my blood which is shed for you." He was "crucified
for us men and our salvation." This is the deep meaning of our sal-
valtion in Christ. Christ suffered as a man on the cross and conquered sin and death for all of humanity. God became man to help
man become God, to help him find his place near God. That is
how much God loved and loves the world! (Jn.3.16).

I Thirst . . . It is Finished
John 19. 28-30

Knowing that his work was finished, Christ said, "I thirst." The
soldiers offered him some wine vinegar as was the custom to those
crucified. Thus Psalm 69:21 which says "They gave me vinegar for
my thirst," was fulfilled. When Christ tasted the vinegar, he said,
"It is finished, and he bowed his head and gave up his spirit," into
the hands of the Father, as Luke adds (23.46). These final words
reveal to us how much in control of himself Christ remained to
the end. Jesus lived his entire life in obedience and love to the Father, and at the end when he completed his work, he bowed his
head and gave up his spirit to the Father. John 10.17-18 reminds
us of these things. Salvation is the work of the Holy Trinity—the
common will and the common love of the Father and the Son fulfilled in the Holy Spirit and in the Church.

Signs at the Death of Christ
Mt. 27.51-54

Matthew records in his gospel that when Christ died there was a great earthquake; the curtain which separated the holy of holies in the temple was torn in two from top to bottom; rocks split and "tombs were opened and many bodies of the saints...were raised, and coming out of the tombs after his resurrection, went into the holy city and appeared to many people" (Mt.27.52-53).

The Removal from the Cross
John 19.31-42; Matthew 27.57-61; Mark 15.52-57; Luke 23.50-54

The day of the crucifixion was Friday, the day of preparation. In three hours the great day of the Sabbath would begin and it was not permissible to leave the bodies on the cross. The soldiers broke the legs of the two men who had been crucified with Jesus to hasten their death. Jesus, however, had already died and they did not need to break his bones. One soldier instead pierced the side of Jesus with his spear, bringing a sudden flow of blood and water—a confirmation that he had already died.

The hour of death was 3:00 P.M., the time when the lambs were slaughtered for the Jewish passover; then John remembered that Jesus was the real Lamb of God, who has borne the sin of the world. The passover lamb of the Jews was a foreshadowed Christ, who was sacrificed to liberate the people not from the Egyptians, but from the tyranny of sin and death. For this reason the bones of Jesus were not broken, as was prescribed by the law for the passover lamb (Ex.12.46; 1Cor.5.7). In the blood and water which flowed from the side of Jesus, John and the Fathers of the Church see two of the sacraments—Baptism and the Holy Eucharist—which sanctify the Church (1 Jn.5.16).

After the death of Jesus the secret disciples appeared. First Joseph of Arimathea, a wealthy member of the Sanhedrin, dared to ask Pilate for the body of Christ. He and Nicodemos prepared the body according to Jewish custom. Because it was late they hurriedly placed the body in a new tomb that was there nearby cut into the rock and they closed the opening with a large stone. The women who were at the cross watched to see his burial also.

The Tomb is Secured
Mt. 27.62-66

The religious instinct of the people in general accepted Jesus as the Messiah-Christ. The leaders of the people, however, led him to the cross and to the tomb. Now they feared Christ even while he was in the tomb. They had heard somehow that Christ might be resurrected on the third day after his death. So they asked the authorities to place a guard of soldiers at the tomb until the third day.

Christ is lying in the tomb. "This is the blessed Sabbath...the day of rest, and on it the only begotten Son of God rested from all his works." Thus was terminated the earthly life of the "Jesus of history"—as certain theologians of our time prefer to know him. With the resurrection begins the other chapter, the chapter of the "Christ of Faith" who will remain forever with us until the end of time. It is in the Christ of faith that we can understand the Jesus of the gospels, for the gospels have been written out of the faith of the Church in the person of Christ.

CHAPTER FOURTEEN

THE RESURRECTION AND ASCENSION

The Resurrection of Christ
John 20.1-31; Matthew 18.1-20;

The four Evangelists preached the miraculous event of the resurrection as an historical event without any further explanation. They all mention the empty tomb and the appearances of the resurrected Christ to his disciples as a reality that does not require further questioning. The commonly used phrases by the Evangelists are: "He is risen, he is not here, he is risen as he said," "Go and tell my disciples" (Mt.28.5-10); "He appeared to Simon" (Lk. 24.34); "I have seen the Lord,...we have seen the Lord" (Jn.20. 18,25); "He appeared to James...he appeared to me also" (1 Cor. 15.3-8).

The appearances of the resurrected Christ are not purely natural nor simply visions as the visions of the prophets. They are perceptible and real appearances of the incarnated and resurrected Christ with his deified or glorified and spiritual body. This is why neither Mary Magdalene nor the two disciples going to Emmaus recognized him immediately, nor even the eleven disciples. In addition the appearances took place according to the ability each person had to recognize Christ. Thus Christ appeared differently to Mary Magdalene and differently to Thomas and to Paul.

The Evangelists chose a few of the appearances and they present them to us as they understood them. As we study the appearances of the resurrected Christ we must not seek to find so much historical sequence and accuracy as the reality of the event of the resurrection itself and how each Evangelist understood and saved that truth to strengthen us in our faith. If we want to see the events of that first Sunday in some related order on the basis of the gospel records, we see them approximately as follows:

The myrrh-bearing women went very early in the morning to anoint the body of Jesus in the tomb. They found that the large stone at the entrance to the tomb was moved to the side. As soon as Mary saw the empty tomb she left immediately to tell Peter and John "they have taken the Lord out of the tomb, and we do not know where they have put him!" Peter and John ran to the tomb (Jn.20.1-3).

In the meantime the other women at the tomb saw the angel who told them that "the Lord is risen." They, too, left directly with fear and great joy to tell the disciples of the joyous event. Mark stops here. For him the good news of the resurrection is enough. The reality of the resurrection itself bears testimony to the rest of the story. On their way to the disciples the women saw the resurrected Christ (Mt.28.1-9). The women brought the good news to the apostles, but the apostles did not believe. "Their words seemed to them as nonsense" (Lk.24.10-11).

Peter and John went into the tomb and saw the burial linens folded and placed neatly in one spot. Then they remembered and believed that Christ had to rise again from the dead, according to the Scriptures. They returned again to the other disciples (Jn.20.3-10). In the meantime Mary Magdalene had returned to the tomb when she saw the angels and Christ himself, and she received the news of the resurrection from the Lord himself in that moving scene described in John 20.11-18.

On the evening of that first Sunday Christ appeared to two men returning to Emmaus. As soon as the two men recognized Christ "at the breaking of the bread" they ran back to Jerusalem to tell the apostles. The apostles had already heard of the resurrection and began to say,"It is true! The Lord has risen and has appeared to Simon. Then the two told what had happened on the way, and

how Jesus was known to them when he broke the bread"
13-35).

In these appearances we can observe that the synoptics speak
somewhat generally and freely. John, however, describes in greater
detail the spiritual experiences he lived on that day. Mary Magdalene was the first to go to the tomb. She took the message of the
empty tomb to Peter and John. Peter and John ran to the tomb.
They believed that Christ had to be resurrected. But their faith did
not appear to have been steadfast at first until they, too, saw the
resurrected Lord personally. When Mary Magdalene saw the Lord
she told the apostles: "I have seen the Lord!"

On the evening of that first Sunday, Christ appeared to his disciples in his body but unbound by space. He entered the room
while the doors were shut. He extended to them the divine greet-
ing of peace: "Peace be with you." The disciples rejoiced. This was
the joy he had promised to them (Jn.14.27,16.20-24). Luke notes
here that the disciples "were startled and frightened, thinking they
saw a ghost...they still did not believe it because of joy and
amazement" (Lk.24.27,41). It was indeed very difficult for anyone to describe their emotions at that time. Christ calmed them
with his peace again and commissioned them to begin the work of
the Church.

"Peace be with you! As the Father has sent me, I am sending
you." And with that he breathed on them and said, "Receive
the Holy Spirit. If you forgive anyone his sins, they are forgiven" (Jn. 20.19-23).

The Confession of Faith By Thomas
John 20.25-31

At the first appearance of Christ Thomas was not with the other
disciples. The ten disciples were telling him, "We have seen the
Lord," but Thomas could not believe. Only if he could see with
his own eyes and touch the wounds with his own hands would he
believe. Eight days later Christ appeared again and with the same
words expressed by Thomas, He called him to faith: "Put your
finger here and see my hands; and put out your hand and place
it in my side; do not be faithless, but stop doubting and believe
(Jn. 20.27). The heart of Thomas leaped with joy and emotion

and he cried out: "My Lord and my God!" From the doubting
Thomas we received the highest and clearest confession of faith in
the person of Christ.

"Blessed Are Those Who Have Not Seen and Yet Have Believed"
John 20.29

Thomas wanted to see, to believe. And the Lord, who knew the
heart of Thomas, gave him that opportunity to see. Thomas indeed saw, believed, and confessed the good confession of faith.
But Christ added the following important comment: Blessed are
those people who will believe in Christ without seeing him with
their natural eyes. God does not always appear in visible form. But
God will always speak to us through the testimony of those who
saw him, and he will always reveal himself to the believing hearts
in a thousand ways. The heart is the point where man meets God
and believes. The greatest sign-event through which God will always speak to us is the cross and the resurrection of Christ – the
unique source of life for the faithful.

Blessed are the hearts that are open, feel the touch of God, and
believe without visible signs. With the confession of faith by Thomas, the gospel is completed. The purpose of the gospel is to help
us to know and to believe that Jesus of Nazareth is the anticipated
Savior-Christ, the Son and Logos of God and who became incarnate and dwelt among us. He was crucified and resurrected for our
own life and our own resurrection. Whoever believes and confesses
him as "Lord and God," as Thomas did, has life eternal (Jn.20.
30-31).

It was with this faith that John wrote the prologue to his gospel
where he testifies to his faith in the person of Christ as it developed from his first meeting with Jesus on the banks of the river
Jordan (Jn.1.40) to the event of the resurrection, and also as it
matured with the experience of Christ over many years in the life
of the Church.

The resurrection of Christ as an historical event is the founda-
tion and source of the Christian faith. Without a positive and concrete faith in the resurrection as a real event one cannot speak

about the Christ of the gospels and of the Church.

The resurrection is the mystery of mysteries and will never fit into the mind of finite man. It is super-natural but not un-natural. It is a matter of faith, a matter of the heart and not of the mind. The Church has made the resurrection an article of faith: I believe "that he was resurrected on the third day, according to the Scriptures" (1 Cor.15.4).

The resurrection as a reality created faith and this faith "overcame the world," and led the world to Christ. The renunciation of the resurrection makes the whole world irrational. Everything remains in darkness, everything becomes the "darkness," which Christ came to illumine (Jn.1.5). With the resurrection "everything is filled with light—the heavens, the earth and the regions below the earth," as the Church sings during Easter (third ode).

The Resurrection Overcomes the Scandal of the Cross

The resurrection illumines the whole work of Christ and particularly the cross of Christ. The first and principal difficulty which the Christian gospel met and continues to meet is the scandal of the cross. Both the Jews and the Gentiles expected a messianic savior. Even to the present day people always long for a dynamic, messianic leader. As long as they could see miracles and marvelous teaching, the Jews were ready to believe in Christ, to proclaim him king and savior. But they could never recognize as messiah a weak person, a crucified person. They all knew how hideous was the expression in Holy Scripture: "cursed is everyone who is hung on a tree. (Gal. 3.13; Deut.27.33). Thus, everyone was scandalized, and some simply because they knew his humble origin in Nazareth. They had actually expected Jesus to come in power from heaven (Jn.1.46,7.27,41). Even Peter who had confessed him as messiah, when he heard about the passion, replied: "May God forbid that you should die such a death." That was when Christ told him, "Go away Satan!" (Mk.8.27-33). When the women brought the message of the resurrection of the crucified Christ many of the disciples did not believe, and "their words seemed to them like nonsense" (Lk.24.11). But when they actually saw Christ for themselves they believed as Thomas believed and confessed the good confession: "My Lord and my God."

Faith in the resurrection really overcame the scandal of the cross. It is to this end that the Evangelists emphasize the empty tomb and the various appearances of the resurrected Christ. The reality of the resurrection made Paul the persecutor into Paul the apostle of Christ. Paul persecuted the Christians precisely because they believed in a crucified messiah, which was inconceivable for his faith. But when the resurrected Christ met Paul, he believed and his kerygma became the cross and the resurrection. With absolute conviction in the resurrection of Christ Paul could write:

We preach Christ crucified...the power of God and the wisdom of God...If Christ had not been raised, your faith is futile... But Christ has indeed been raised from the dead, the first fruits of those who have fallen asleep (1 Cor.1.22-24,15.12-23).

The Cross in the Light of the Resurrection

Without the light of the resurrection, the cross of Christ with those last words: "My God, my God, why have you forsaken me?" "Father forgive them," and "It is finished," remains a dark mystery. Only the reality of the resurrection has convinced us that "it was meant for Christ to suffer and then enter his glory" (Lk.24. 25,46; Phil.2.8-11; Heb. 2.9). Through the resurrection we learn that the cross was within the eternal plan of God for the salvation of the world, and was not a fortuitous and unexpected event. Christ had been destined from eternity to die for the salvation of the world. "For God so loved the world that he gave his one and only Son, that whosoever believes in him shall not perish but have eternal life" (Jn.16; Rom.3.25; Eph.3.8-15).

The death of Christ on the cross is the greatest miracle of the Triune God by which he abolished the power of death and brought man, who was suffering alone apart from God, once again near to God. The resurrection, as the fruit of the cross, is the triumph of the loving God against evil; it is the victory of life over corruption and death which reigned in the world because of sin. The resurrection is the recall of nature to its original condition; it testifies that life is above the corruption and death which sin had introduced to the world. The believer in Christ and in his resurrection "does not die but passes from death into life." In the resurrection we celebrate the death of death. This is precisely how the resurrection of Christ is depicted in the Byzantine icon — as destroying the kingdom of hades.

The Resurrection is a Recreating and Transfiguring Power

The resurrection of Christ is understood as the energy of God recreating the world. With the resurrection a new creation came into being; a new life was inaugurated in which new powers are at work. The "power of the resurrection" is the power of divine grace which transfigures, sanctifies and makes all believers sons and daughters of God. The first transfiguration and *theosis* was accomplished in the human nature of Christ. The same divine power which worked the resurrection of Christ also works the spiritual resurrection and rebirth of the faithful. "By his power God raised the Lord from the dead, and he will raise us also" (1 Cor.6.14; Rom.8.11; Eph. 1.19-20,3.7).

Life as we see it will have its great questions, but we will only find the answer in steadfast faith in the resurrection of Christ and in the hope of our own resurrection. This hope of our own resurrection helps us to carry our own small cross of life with the satisfaction of knowing that we are "co-workers with God." "If we suffer with him we shall also be glorified with him" (Rom.8.17).

The Ascension of Chirst
Acts 1.1-12; Lk. 24.49-53

For forty days the resurrected Christ appeared bodily to his disciples to strengthen them in faith and to prepare them for their apostolic work. He promised that he would send them the Holy Spirit, as power from heaven, to help them carry out their missionary work. On the fortieth day Christ led his disciples out to Bethany. There he first blessed them and then he ascended into heaven.

When he had led them out to the vicinity of Bethany, he lifted up his hands and blessed them. While he was blessing them, he left them and was taken up into heaven (Lk.24.49-51). ...He was taken up before their eyes, and a cloud hid him from their sight (Acts 1.9).

This was his final bodily appearance after the resurrection.

In the language of religion the term "heaven" denotes the sphere of the spiritual, the abode of God. Heaven remains the symbol and the place of everything that is truly sublime and divine. the cloud expresses the glory of God. Christ ascended to heaven at the right hand of God the Father. And from there "every perfect gift" comes down to us from "the Father of lights." From there he sends us the Holy Spirit and all the spiritual gifts which the mind of man cannot imagine and the tongue of man cannot express. Only the heart which believes understands them and expresses them with symbols which are familiar to it (Jas.1.17; Eph.4. 10-26; 1 Cor.2.9-10).

It is possible to say that the bodily appearances during the forty days after the resurrection belong to the earthly life of Christ. The ascension as the last bodily appearance of the resurrected Christ was the climax of the divine economy of the incarnation. With the ascension, the entire work of the incarnation was completed. Christ came from the Father in heaven; he became man and lived among us; he taught and worked miracles; he suffered on the cross for our sins; he was resurrected and by divine economy appeared bodily to his disciples. Finally, he ascended into heaven, to the Father to receive the glory he had with the Father before the world was created (Jn.17.5,24). From there in heaven he reigns over his Church, and as a forerunner he calls us all to follow him (Heb.6. 20, 1 Cor.15.22-28; Phil.2.9-11).

EPILOGUE

This is the person and the work of Christ as the eyewitnesses, the apostles, saw him in his earthly life, and as they have tried to present him to us in their gospels.

They saw him as true man, "the son of David, the son of Abraham," "born of a woman," growing and becoming strong, filled with wisdom, and the favor of God was upon him. And yet he always appeared as being something more than man. Something unique, awesome and mysterious was hidden in his person. A sacred, divine power flowed from him and affected everyone in his presence.

He taught about God and his will, but his teaching was unique. He taught not like a God-fearing rabbi; he taught with a unique authority. He was the Word of God itself, as John said.

His relationship with God was unique. He was the Son of God in a unique way; he was the *monogenis* the only Son of God. For Christ the will of God was not just a commandment to be obeyed; it was his food, his life. The will of God was the will of Christ. Christ was ready to die and he died for the will of God. Christ came to do, to realize the will of God. Christ is the will of God incarnate for the salvation of the world.

The theme of his teaching was love. But his love was unique. He loved everyone. He made the pain and the burden of people his own pain and burden. He loved us "to the end;" he laid down his life for his friends. Christ was the love of God incarnate for our salvation, "that is, God was in Christ reconciling the world to himself" (Jn.3.16; 2Cor.5.19-21).

The person of Christ belongs to the mystery of God and the world. Christ is the Son of God, who became the Son of Man to serve and give his life as a ransom for many. The "many" did not understand, did not accept him, for the mystery of God is revealed only to those who have opened their hearts to God. John expresses this complaint throughout his gospel (1.5,10-12,12.37-43,15. 22-25).

John, especially in his mature faith and love has understood the depth of the person of Christ and it is John who says the last word on him. Christ is the Logos, and the Logos was God. . .all things were made through him . . . and the Logos became flesh and dwelled among us, full of grace and truth . . . and from his fullness have we all received...he is our Lord and our God (1.1-18,20.30-31).

The Son of God became man; he died for us; he is risen and ascended to heaven. There he waits for us to follow him in the new life of resurrection. How we can follow the resurrected Christ in heaven will be the subject of the second volume of this work. There we will see how the Church, guided by the holy Spirit, has understood the person and work of our Lord; how the believers, in the power of the Holy Spirit, live their lives in Christ in faith, love, prayer, worship, and in anticipation of his Second Coming, when we shall be with him for ever in his heavenly and everlasting kingdom (Lk.22.27-30; Jn.17.24; 1 Thess. 4.17).

INDEX TO OLD TESTAMENT REFERENCES